Harvar
Business
Review

McKINSEY AWARD WINNERS

THE HARVARD BUSINESS REVIEW PAPERBACK SERIES

The series is designed to bring today's managers and professionals the fundamental information they need to stay competitive in a fast-moving world. From the preeminent thinkers whose work has defined an entire field to the rising stars who will redefine the way we think about business, here are the leading minds and landmark ideas that have established the *Harvard Business Review* as required reading for ambitious businesspeople in organizations around the globe.

Other books in the series:

Harvard Business Review Interviews with CEOs

Harvard Business Review on Advances in Strategy

Harvard Business Review on Appraising Employee Performance

Harvard Business Review on Becoming a High Performance Manager

Harvard Business Review on Brand Management

Harvard Business Review on Breakthrough Leadership

Harvard Business Review on Breakthrough Thinking

Harvard Business Review on Bringing Your Whole Self to Work

Harvard Business Review on Building Personal and Organizational Resilience

Harvard Business Review on the Business Value of IT

Harvard Business Review on CEO Succession

Harvard Business Review on Change

Harvard Business Review on Collaborating Across Silos

Harvard Business Review on Compensation

Harvard Business Review on Corporate Ethics

Harvard Business Review on Corporate Governance

Harvard Business Review on Corporate Responsibility

Harvard Business Review on Corporate Strategy

Harvard Business Review on Crisis Management

Other books in the series (continued):

Other books in the series (continued):

Harvard Business Review

McKINSEY AWARD WINNERS

A HARVARD BUSINESS REVIEW PAPERBACK

ISBN: 978-1-4221-6697-0

Library-of-Congress cataloging information forthcoming

The paper used in this publication meets the requirements of the
American National Standard for Permanence of Paper for Publications
and Documents in Libraries and Archives Z39.48-1992.

Table of Contents

Harvard
Business
Review
McKINSEY AWARD WINNERS

Good Managers Don't Make Policy Decisions

H. EDWARD WRAPP

Executive Summary

THIS ARTICLE WAS first published in the September–October 1967 issue. The editors have chosen it as an "HBR Classic" because it has passed the test of time with flying colors. Requests for reprints still come in at an impressive rate.

The article's continued success is all the more remarkable because in the 1960s its precepts of good management were heretical. The author's successful general manager is an opportunist and a muddler who does not spell out detailed company objectives or master plans, one who seldom makes forthright statements of policy, one who often gets personally involved in operating matters.

In a retrospective commentary, the author discusses putting his theories into practice, and points out the reasons why managers—even those who have tried to follow his precepts of good management—have been swept over the dam.

Mr. Wrapp retired in 1983 as professor of business policy at the Graduate School of Business, University of Chicago, a position he had held for 20 years. He also was director of the school's executive program and associate dean for management programs. He has served on the boards of numerous corporations.

T HE UPPER REACHES OF MANAGEMENT are a land of mystery and intrigue. Very few people have ever been there, and the present inhabitants frequently send back messages that are incoherent both to other levels of management and to the world in general.

This absence of firsthand reports may account for the myths, illusions, and caricatures that permeate the literature of management—for example, such widely held notions as these:

- Life gets less complicated as a manager reaches the top of the pyramid.

- Managers at the top level know everything that's going on in the organization, can command whatever resources they may need, and therefore can be more decisive.

- The general manager's day is taken up with making broad policy decisions and formulating precise objectives.

- The top executive's primary activity is conceptualizing long-range plans.

- In a large company, the top executive may meditate about the role of his or her organization in society.

I suggest that none of these versions alone, or in combination, is an accurate portrayal of what a general manager does. Perhaps students of the management process have been overly eager to develop a theory and a discipline. As one executive I know puts it, "I guess I do some of the things described in the books and articles, but the descriptions are lifeless, and my job isn't."

What common characteristics, then, do successful executives exhibit in reality? I shall identify five skills or talents which, in my experience, seem especially significant.

Keeping Well Informed

First, each of my heroes has a special talent for keeping informed about a wide range of operating decisions being made at different levels in the company. As they move up the ladder, they develop a network of information sources in many different departments. They cultivate these sources and keep them open no matter how high they climb in the organization. When the need arises, they bypass the lines on the organization chart to seek more than one version of a situation.

In some instances, especially when they suspect a manager would not be in total agreement with their decision, subordinates will elect to inform him or her in advance, before they announce a decision. In these circumstances, the manager may defer the decision, redirect it, or even block further action. However, the manager does not insist on this procedure. Ordinarily the members of the organization will decide at what stage to inform the manager.

Top-level managers are frequently criticized by writers, consultants, and lower management for continuing to enmesh themselves in operating problems rather than withdrawing to the "big picture." Without doubt, some managers do get lost in a welter of detail and insist on making too many decisions. Superficially, the good manager may seem to make the same mistake—but for different purposes. Only by keeping well informed about the decisions being made can the good manager avoid the sterility so often found in those who isolate themselves from operations. If she or he follows the advice to free her or himself from operations, the general manager may soon subsist on a diet of abstractions, leaving the choice of food in the hands of subordinates. As Kenneth Boulding put it, "The very purpose of a hierarchy is to prevent information from reaching higher layers. It operates as an information filter, and there are little wastebaskets all along the way."[1]

What kinds of action does a successful executive take to ensure that information is live and accurate? One company president that I worked with, for example, sensed that his vice presidents were insulating him from some of the vital issues being discussed at lower levels. He accepted a proposal for a formal management development program primarily because it afforded him an opportunity to discuss company problems with middle managers several layers removed from him in the organization. By meeting with small groups of these managers in an academic setting, he learned much about their preoccupations, and also about those of his vice presidents.

And he accomplished his purposes without undermining the authority of line managers.

Focusing Time and Energy

The second skill of the good manager is knowing how to save energy and hours for those few particular issues, decisions, or problems which require personal attention. He or she knows the fine and subtle distinction between keeping fully informed about operating decisions and allowing the organization to force him or her into participating in these decisions or, even worse, making them. Recognizing that special talents can only bear on a limited number of matters, the good manager chooses issues that will have the greatest long-term impact on the company, and on which he or she can be most productive. Under ordinary circumstances, the limit is three or four major objectives during any single period of sustained activity.

What about the situations in which he or she elects *not* to become involved as a decision maker? The managers make sure (using the skill first mentioned) that the organization keeps them informed at various stages; they don't want to be accused of indifference to such issues. They train subordinates not to bring the matters to them for a decision. The communication from below becomes essentially one of: "Here is our sizeup, and here's what we propose to do."

Reserving hearty encouragement for those projects which hold superior promise of a contribution to total corporate strategy, the superior manager acknowledges receipt of information on other matters. When a problem comes from the organization, he or she finds a way to transmit know-how short of giving orders—usually by asking perceptive questions.

Playing the Power Game

To what extent do successful top executives push their ideas and proposals through the organization? The common notion that the "prime mover" continually creates and forces through new programs, like a powerful majority leader in a liberal Congress, is in my opinion very misleading.

The successful manager is sensitive to the power structure in the organization. In considering any major current proposals he can plot the position of various individuals and units in the organization on a scale ranging from complete, outspoken support down to determined, sometimes bitter, and often well-cloaked opposition. In the middle of the scale is indifference. Usually, several aspects of a proposal will fall into this area, and here the manager operates. By assessing the depth and nature of blocks in the organization, the manager can move through what I call corridors of comparative indifference. He or she seldom challenges a blocked corridor, preferring to pause until it has opened up.

Related to this particular skill is the ability to recognize when a few trial balloon launches are needed in the organization. The organization will tolerate only a certain number of proposals which emanate from the apex of the pyramid, so no matter how great the temptation to stimulate the organization with a flow of personal ideas, the good manager knows he or she must work through others in different parts of the organization. Studying the reactions of key individuals and groups to the trial balloons these persons send up, the manager can better assess how to limit the emasculation of proposals. There is seldom a proposal which is supported by all quarters of the organization. The emergence of strong support in certain quarters is almost sure to evoke strong opposition in others.

SENSE OF TIMING

Circumstances like these mean that a good sense of timing is a priceless asset for a top executive. For example, a vice president had for some time been convinced that her company lacked a sense of direction and needed a formal long-range planning activity to fill the void. Up to the time in question, her soft overtures to other top executives had been rebuffed. And then she spotted an opening.

A management development committee proposed a series of weekend meetings for second-level officers in the company. After extensive debate, but for reasons not announced, the president rejected this proposal. The members of the committee openly resented what seemed to them an arbitrary rejection.

The vice president, sensing a tense situation, suggested to the president that the same officers who were to have attended the weekend management development seminars be organized into a long-range planning committee. The timing was perfect. The president, looking for a bone to toss to the committee, acquiesced immediately, and the management development committee in its next meeting enthusiastically endorsed the idea.

This vice president had been conducting a kind of continuing market research to discover how to sell her long-range planning proposal. Her previous probes of the "market" had told her that the president's earlier rejections of the proposal were not so final as to preclude an eventual shift in the "corridors of attitude."

The vice president caught the committee in a concil-
iatory mood, and her proposal rode through with flying
colors.

CAUTIOUS PRESSURE

As good managers stand at a point in time, they can
identify a set of goals, albeit pretty hazy. Their timeta-
bles, also pretty hazy, suggest that some goals must be
accomplished sooner than others, and that others may
be safely postponed for several months or years. They
have a still hazier notion of how to reach these goals.
They assess key individuals and groups. They know that
each has its own set of goals, some of which they thoroughly understand and others about which they can only
speculate. They know also that these individuals and
groups represent blocks to certain programs or projects,
and that as points of opposition, they must be taken into
account. As day-to-day operating decisions are made,
and as both individuals and groups respond to proposals,
it is more clear where the corridors of comparative indifference are. The manager takes action accordingly.

Appearing Imprecise

The fourth skill of the successful manager is knowing
how to satisfy the organization so that it has a sense of
direction without ever actually committing publicly to a
specific set of objectives. This is not to say that he or she
does not have better objectives—personal and corporate,
long-term and short-term. They are significant guides to
thinking, and the successful manager modifies them
continually while gaining a better understanding of the
resources, the competition, and the changing market

demands. But as the organization clamors for statements of objectives, these are samples of what it gets back:

"Our company aims to be number one in its industry."

"Our objective is growth with profit."

"We seek the maximum return on investment."

"Management's goal is to meet its responsibilities to stockholders, employees, and the public."

In my opinion, statements such as these provide almost no guidance to the various levels of management. Yet they are quire readily accepted as objectives by large numbers of intelligent people.

MAINTAIN VIABILITY

Why does the good manager shy away from precise statements of objectives for the organization? The main reason is that specific objectives will not be relevant for any reasonable period into the future. Conditions in business change continually and rapidly, and corporate strategy must be revised to take the changes into account. The more explicit the statement of strategy, the more difficult it becomes to persuade the organization to turn to different goals when needs and conditions shift.

The public and the stockholders, to be sure, must perceive the organization as having a well-defined set of objectives and a clear sense of direction. But in reality the good top manager is seldom so certain of the direction which should be taken. Better than anyone else, he or she senses many, many threats to the company— threats which lie in the economy, in the actions of competitors, and, not least, within the organization.

The good manager also knows that it is impossible to state objectives clearly enough so that everyone in the organization understands what they mean. Objectives only get communicated over time by consistency or pattern in operating decisions. Such decisions are more meaningful than words. When precise objectives are spelled out, the organization tends to interpret them so they fit its own needs.

Subordinates who keep pressing for more precise objectives are working against their own best interests. Each time objectives are stated more specifically, a subordinate's range of possibilities for operating are reduced. The narrower field means less room to roam and to accommodate the flow of ideas coming up from his or her part of the organization.

AVOID POLICY STRAITJACKETS

The successful manager's reluctance to be precise extends into the area of policy decisions. He or she seldom makes a forthright statement of policy, aware perhaps that in some companies executives spend more time arbitrating disputes caused by stated policies than in moving the company forward. Management textbooks contend that well-defined policies are the sine qua non of a well-managed company. My research does not bear out this contention.

For example, the president of one company with which I am familiar deliberately leaves assignments of his top officers vague and refuses to define policies for them. He passes out new assignments seemingly with no pattern in mind and consciously sets up competitive ventures among his subordinates. His methods, though they would never be sanctioned by a classical organization planner, are deliberate—and, incidentally, quite effective.

Since able managers do not make policy decisions, does this mean that well-managed companies operate without policies? Certainly not. But their policies evolve over time from an indescribable mix of operating decisions. From any single operating decision might have come a very minor dimension of the policy as the organization understands it; from a series of decisions comes a pattern of guidelines for various levels of the organization.

The skillful manager resists the urge to write a company creed or to compile a policy manual. Preoccupation with detailed statements of corporate objectives, and departmental goals and with comprehensive organization charts and job descriptions is often the first symptom of an organization in the first stages of atrophy.

The "management by objectives" school, so widely heralded in recent years, suggests that detailed objectives be spelled out at all levels in the corporation. This method is feasible at lower levels of management, but it becomes unworkable at the upper levels. The top manager must think out objectives in detail, but withhold some or at least communicate them to the organization in modest doses. A conditioning process which may stretch out over months or years is necessary to prepare the organization for radical departures from what it is currently striving to attain.

Suppose, for example, that a president is convinced the company must phase out of the principal business it has been in for 35 years. Although making this change is one of his objectives, he may well feel that he cannot disclose the idea to even his vice presidents, whose total know-how is in the present business. A blunt announcement that the company is changing horses would be too great a shock, so he begins moving toward this goal without a full disclosure to his management group.

Spelling out objectives in detail may only complicate the task of reaching them. Specific statements give the opposition an opportunity to organize its defenses.

Muddling with a Purpose

The fifth and most important skill I shall describe bears little relation to the doctrine that management is (or should be) a comprehensive, systematic, logical, well-programmed science. Of all the heresies set forth here, this should strike doctrinaires as the rankest!

The successful manager, in my observation, recognizes the futility of trying to push total packages or programs through the organization. He or she is willing to take less than total acceptance in order to achieve modest progress toward goals. Avoiding debates on principles, he or she tries to piece together parts that may appear to be incidental into a program that moves at least part of the way toward the objectives. Optimistic and persistent, the good manager says over and over, "There must be some parts of this proposal on which we can capitalize."

Relationships among different proposals present opportunities for combination and restructuring. It follows that the manager has wide-ranging interests and curiosity. The more things she knows about, the more opportunities she will have to discover parts which are related. This process does not require great intellectual brilliance or unusual creativity. The wider ranging her interests, the more likely that she will be able to tie together several unrelated proposals. The good manager is skilled as an analyst, but even more talented as a conceptualizer.

If the manager has built or inherited a solid organization, it will be difficult to come up with an idea which no one in the company has ever thought of before. The most significant contribution may be to see relationships that no one else has seen.

A division manager, for example, had set as one objective at the start of a year, an improvement in product quality. At the end of the year, reviewing progress toward this objective, she could identify three significant events which had brought about a perceptible improvement.

First, the head of the quality control group, a veteran manager who was doing only an adequate job, had asked early in the year for assignment to a new research group. The division manager installed a promising young engineer in this key spot.

A few months later, opportunity number two came along. The personnel department proposed a continuous program of checking the effectiveness of training methods for new employees. The proposal was acceptable to the manufacturing group. The division manager's only contribution was to suggest that the program should include a heavy emphasis on employees' attitudes toward quality.

A third opportunity arose when one of the division's best customers discovered that the wrong material had been used for a large lot of parts. The heat this generated made it possible to institute a completely new system of procedures for inspecting and testing raw materials.

As the division manager reviewed the year's progress on product quality, these were the three most important developments. None of these developments could have been predicted at the start of the year, but she was quick to see the potential in each when it popped up in the day-to-day operating routines.

EXPLOITING CHANGE

The good manager can function effectively only in an environment of continual change. A *Saturday Review* cartoonist caught the idea when he pictured an executive seated at a massive desk instructing his secretary to "send in a deal; I feel like wheelin'." Only the manager with many changes in the works can discover new combinations of opportunities and open up new corridors of comparative indifference. His or her creative stimulation comes from trying to make something useful of the proposal or idea on the desk. He will try to make strategic change a way of life in the organization and continually review the strategy even though current results are good.

Charles Lindblom wrote an article with an engaging title, "The Science of Muddling Through."[2] He described what he called "the rational comprehensive method" of decision making. The essence of this method is that for every problem the decision maker proceeds deliberately, one step at a time, to collect complete data; to analyze the data thoroughly; to study a wide range of alternatives, each with its own risks and consequences; and, finally, to formulate a detailed course of action. Lindblom immediately dismissed "the rational comprehensive method" in favor of what he called "successive limited comparisons." He saw a decision maker comparing the alternatives in order to learn which most closely meets the objectives he or she has in mind. Since this is an opportunistic process, he saw the manager as a muddler, but a muddler with a purpose.

H. Igor Ansoff, in his book, *Corporate Strategy*, espoused a similar notion in what he described as the "cascade approach."[3] In his view, possible decision rules are formulated in gross terms and are successively refined through several stages as the emergence of a solution proceeds. This process gives the appearance of solving the problem several times over, but with successively more precise results:

Both Lindblom and Ansoff moved us closer to an understanding of how managers really think. The process is not abstract; rather, the manager searches for a means of drawing into a pattern the thousands of incidents which make up the day-to-day life of a growing company.

CONTRASTING PICTURES

It is interesting to note, in the writings of students of management, the emergence of the concept that, rather than making decisions, the leader's principal task is to maintain operating conditions that permit the various decision-making systems to function effectively. Supporters of this theory, it seems to me, overlook the subtle turns of direction which the leader can provide. The leader cannot add purpose and structure to the balanced judgments of subordinates by simply rubber-stamping their decisions. He or she must weigh the issues and reach his or her own decisions.

Richard M. Cyert and James G. March contend that real-life managers do not consider all possible courses of action, that their search ends with one satisfactory alternative. In my sample, good managers are not guilty of such myopic thinking. Unless they mull over a wide range of possibilities, they cannot come up with the imaginative combinations of ideas which characterize their work.

Many of the articles about successful executives picture them as great thinkers who sit at their desks drafting master blueprints for their companies. The successful top executives I have seen at work do not operate this way. Rather than produce a full-grown decision tree, they start with a twig, help it grow, and ease themselves out on the limbs only after they have tested to see how much weight the limbs can stand.

In my picture, the general manager sits in the midst of a continuous stream of operating problems. The organization presents a flow of proposals to deal with the problems. Some of these proposals are contained in voluminous, well-documented, formal reports; some are as fleeting as the walk-in visit from a subordinate whose latest inspiration came during the morning's coffee break. Knowing how meaningless it is to say, "This is a finance problem," or, "That is a communications problem," the manager feels no compulsion to classify them. As Gary Steiner, in one of his speeches, put it, "He has a high tolerance for ambiguity."

In considering each proposal, the general manager tests it against at least three criteria:

1. Will the total proposal—or, more often, will some part of the proposal—move the organization toward the objectives in mind?

2. How will the whole or parts of the proposal be received by the various groups and subgroups in the organization? Where will the strongest opposition come from, which group will furnish the strongest support, and which group will be neutral or indifferent?

3. How does the proposal relate to programs already in process or currently proposed? Can some parts of the proposal under consideration be added on to a program already under way, or can they be combined

with all or parts of other proposals in a package
which can be steered through the organization?

THE MAKING OF A DECISION

As another example of a general manager at work, consider the train of events which led to a parent company
president's decision to attempt to consolidate two of his
divisions.

Let us call the executive Mr. Brown. One day the
manager of Division A came to him with a proposal that
Division A acquire a certain company. That company's
founder and president—let us call him Mr. Johansson—
had a phenomenal record of inventing new products, but
earnings had been less than phenomenal. Johansson's
asking price for his company was high when evaluated
against the earnings record.

Not until Brown began to speculate on how Johansson
might supply fresh vigor for new products in Division A
did it appear that perhaps a premium price could be jus-
tified. For several years, Brown had been unsuccessful in
stimulating the manager of that division to see that she
must bring in new products to replace those that were
losing their place in the market.

The next idea that came to Brown was that Johansson
might invent not only for Division A but also for Division
B. As Brown analyzed how this could work out organizationally, he began to think about the markets being
served by Divisions A and B. Over the years, several basic
but gradual changes in marketing patterns had occurred,
and the marketing considerations that had dictated the
establishment of separate divisions no longer prevailed.
Why should the company continue to support dupli-
cated overhead expenses in the two divisions?

As Brown weighed the issues, he concluded that by consolidating the two divisions he could also shift responsibilities in the management groups in ways that would strengthen them overall. If we were asked to evaluate Brown's capabilities, how would we respond? Putting aside the objection that the information is too sketchy, our tendency might be to criticize Brown. Why did he not identify the changing market patterns in his continuing review of company position? Why did he not force the issue when the division manager failed to do something about new product development? Such criticism would reflect "the rational comprehensive method" of decision making.

But, as I analyze the gyrations in Brown's thinking, one characteristic stands out. He kept searching for follow-on opportunities from the original proposal, opportunities that would stand up against the three criteria earlier mentioned. In my book, Brown rates as an extremely skillful general manager.

Conclusion

To recapitulate, the general manager possesses five important skills. He or she knows how to:

1. **Keep open many pipelines of information.** No one will quarrel with the desirability of an early warning system that provides varied viewpoints on an issue. However, very few managers know how to practice this skill, and the books on management add precious little to our understanding of the techniques that make it practicable.

2. **Concentrate on a limited number of significant issues.** No matter how skillful the manager is in

focusing his energies and talents, he is inevitably caught up in a number of inconsequential duties. Active leadership of an organization demands a high level of personal involvement, and personal involvement brings with it many time-consuming activities that have an infinitesimal impact on corporate strategy. Hence this second skill, while perhaps the most logical of the five, is by no means the easiest to apply.

3. **Identify the corridors of comparative indifference.** Are there inferences here that the good manager has no ideas of his or her own, that he or she stands by until the organization proposes solutions, that he or she never uses his or her authority to force a proposal through the organization? Such inferences are not intended. The message is that a good organization will tolerate only so much direction from the top; the good manager therefore is adept at sensing how hard to push.

4. **Give the organization a sense of direction with open-ended objectives.** In assessing this skill, keep in mind that I am talking about top levels of management. At lower levels, the manager should be encouraged to write down his or her objectives, if for no other reason than to ascertain if they are consistent with corporate strategy.

5. **Spot opportunities and relationships in the stream of operating problems and decisions.** Lest it be concluded from the description of this skill that the good manager is more an improviser than a planner, let me emphasize that he or she is a planner and encourages planning by his or her subordinates. Interestingly, though, professional planners may be

irritated by a good general manager. Most of them complain about the manager's lack of vision. They devise a master plan, but the president (or other operating executive) seems to ignore it, or to give it minimum acknowledgment by borrowing bits and pieces for implementation. They seem to feel that the power of a good master plan will be obvious to everyone, and its implementation automatic. But the general manager knows that even if the plan is sound and imaginative, the job has only begun. The long, painful task of implementation will depend on his skill, not that of the planner.

If this analysis of how skillful general managers think and operate has validity, then it should help us see several problems in a better light. For instance, the investment community is increasingly interested in sizing up the management of a company being appraised. Thus far, the analysts rely mainly on results or performance rather than on probes of management skills. But current performance can be affected by many variables, both favorable and unfavorable, and is a dangerous base for predicting what the management of a company will produce in the future. Testing the key managers of a company against the five skills described holds promise for evaluating the caliber of a management group. The manager who is building a company and the one who is moving up through the hierarchy of a larger organization require essentially the same capabilities for success.

In today's frenzy of acquisitions and mergers, why does a management usually prefer to acquire a company rather than to develop a new product and build an organization to make and sell it? One of the reasons can be found in the way a general manager thinks and operates.

A general manager finds it difficult to sit and speculate theoretically about the future as he or she and his or her subordinates fashion a plan to exploit a new product. General managers are much more at home when taking over a going concern, even though they anticipate they will inherit many things they do not want. In the day-to-day operation of a going concern, general mangers find the milieu to maneuver and conceptualize.

Scarcely any managers in any business can escape the acutely painful responsibility to identify people with potential for growth in management and to devise methods for developing them for broader responsibilities. Few line managers or staff professionals have genuine confidence in the yardsticks and devices they use now. The five skills offer possibilities for raising an additional set of questions about management appraisal methods, job rotation practices, on-the-job development assignments, and the curricula of formal in-house management development programs.

One group of distinguished executives ignores with alarming regularity the implications of the five skills. These are the presidents of multidivision companies who "promote" successful division managers to the parent company level as staff officers. Does this recurring phenomenon cast doubt on the validity of my theory? I think not. To the contrary, strong supporting evidence for my thesis can be found in the results of such action. What happens is that line managers thus "promoted" often end up on the sidelines, out of the game for the rest of their careers. Removed from the tumult of operations, the environment that I contend is critical for their success, many of them just wither away in their high-status posts as senior counselors and never become effective.

Notes

1. From a speech at a meeting sponsored by the Crowell Collier Institute of Continuing Education in New York, as reported in *Business Week*, February 18, 1967, p. 202.

2. Harold J. Leavitt and Louis R. Pondy, ed., *Readings in Managerial Psychology* (Chicago: University of Chicago Press, 1964), p. 61.

3. H. Igor Ansoff, *Corporate Strategy* (New York: McGraw-Hill, 1965.)

Research

I HAVE REACHED the conclusions outlined here after working closely with many managers in many different companies. In truth, the managers were not preselected with research in mind. Never did I tell the manager that he or she was being studied, nor was I in fact studying his or her behavior. Research was not the purpose of our relationship. We were collaborating to solve some real problem.

Researching the management process when the manager is aware that he or she is being studied sometimes produces strange results. Rarely is a good executive able to think objectively about the management process as it is exemplified in his or her own methods. When managers try to explain to a researcher or writer, they tend to feel compelled to develop rational, systematic explanations of how they do their jobs—explanations that in my opinion are largely fictional.

A manager cannot be expected to describe his or her methods even if he or she understands them. They border on manipulation, and the stigma associated with manipulation can be fatal. If the organization ever identifies the manager as a manipulator, the manager's job becomes more difficult. No one willingly submits to manipulation, and those around the manager organize to protect themselves. And yet every good manager does have to manipulate.

My definition of a good manager is a simple one: under competitive industry conditions, a good manager is able to move his or her organization significantly toward the goals he or she has set, whether measured by higher return on investment, product improvement, development of management talent, faster growth in sales and earnings, or some other standard. Bear in mind that this definition does not refer to the administrator whose principal role is to maintain the status quo in a company or in a department. Keeping the wheels turning in a direction already set is a relatively simple task, compared with that of directing the introduction of a continuing flow of changes and innovations, and preventing the organization from flying apart under pressure.

Retrospective Commentary: A Muddler Looks Back

SELECTION OF "GOOD MANAGERS Don't Make Policy Decisions" as an HBR Classic is a posthumous honor for my strategy course at the

University of Chicago. The article was an attempt
to describe that course's philosophy of management over some 20 years and I probably would
never have written it but for the insistence of
George Shultz, then dean of the business school.
After sitting in on several classes, he urged me to
publish the conclusions drawn from the case discussions. I was reluctant, for it seemed to me that once
the "answers" had been disclosed, future discussions of the cases would be perfunctory. But as it
turned out, distributing the published article in my
classes improved the quality of case discussions.

I remember that I gave an early draft to three
friends for their comments. One, a widely read,
successful CEO, called me the same day to say,
"This is the first thing I have ever read that accu-
rately describes what I do." The other two,
respected academicians, were able to manage at
best a pair of stifled yawns. This was to be the pattern of responses to the article over the years—
widespread support from experienced general
managers and a high level of skepticism from staff
managers and teachers of management.

Since the article's publication in 1967, the pressures to establish financial goals, both short- and
long-term, have increased many-fold, despite the
difficulties of persuading organizations to rally
around a cause defined in quantitative terms. This
has made management's job more difficult, and
has increased my conviction that successful organizations revolve around good general managers.
As I noted in the mid-1970s:

"An organization is doomed to mediocrity unless
it is guided by good general managers in key

positions. A company can bumble along for years, but good general managers are the ingredient which will make it stand out from the pack. No matter how rich its other resources such as technical know-how, uniqueness of product, market monopoly, ample finances, or luck, an organization will not excel unless it is led by what are becoming increasingly rare individuals.

"Generally, it is a good general manager, not the staff specialist, who makes a company go, who turns an idea into a commercial success or converts a major disappointment into an opportunity which catches fire."[1]

Second Thoughts

The heart of the HBR article was the following paragraph from the section "Muddling with a purpose":

"The good manager can function effectively only in an environment of continual change . . . Only with many changes in the works can the manager discover new combinations of opportunities and open up new corridors of comparative indifference. His stimulation to creativity comes from trying to make something useful of the proposal or idea in front of him. He will try to make strategic change a way of life in the organization and continually review the strategy even though the current results are good."

In retrospect, I feel that two points need qualification:

- The beneficial effect of "continual change" does not extend to frequent reorganizations of the management structure. These are among the most damaging abuses that so-called professional managers can inflict on a company. Unless executives' working relationships are reasonably stable, overall performance will suffer. The general manager who listens to organization planning staff views on such matters will almost certainly embark on a rash of ill-advised reorganizations.

- A continual review of strategy should go on only in the general manager's mind, for repeated questioning of strategy by subordinates would introduce too much uncertainty. The organization must stay the course long enough to demonstrate whether the strategy that it is attempting to implement will work. Only the general manager is continually on tenterhooks wondering whether to pause and reevaluate, or to forge ahead.

I would also like to add a qualification to the opening statement of a paragraph in the section, "Appearing Imprecise," that "the fourth skill of the general manager is knowing how to satisfy the organization that it has a sense of direction without ever actually getting himself committed publicly to a specific set of objectives." The annual planning process is an exception to this generalization. Detailed and specific one-year plans can be useful to the general manager who is committed to the spirit of imprecision. As John J. Byrne, the CEO who took Geico Corporation from the verge of bankruptcy to a string of noteworthy successes, has observed, "In the annual plan, the organization needs to know where the goal line is. What does it take to make a touchdown?"

Proof of the Pudding

The basic ideas of this article have been validated in several ways. Although selective perception may be at work, a procession of books and articles published since 1967 supports my findings on the skills of the general manager and the working environment in which he or she can thrive.

My personal sample of general managers has grown to include several dozen with different management styles and varying degrees of success. Some, managing in the mode of the article, have succeeded dramatically. But some have failed. Most companies' methods of selecting and grooming general managers continue to be woefully inadequate and the turnover in general management positions is frighteningly high. Many who tried to emulate my good manager have been swept over the dam, for one or a number of reasons:

Some took over businesses that had deteriorated beyond salvage.

Some drowned in a stream of operating decisions.

Some were sacked because they could not produce immediate profit turnarounds.

Some were immobilized by staff specialists.

Some kept searching for the right management consultant to tell them what to do.

Some simply lacked sufficient company and industry know-how to establish a credible sense of direction.

Some were too greedy.

Literally hundreds of students in advanced management programs have put the article to good test. Those who read it quickly invariably found themselves trapped by a superficial interpretation that collapsed in the face of challenges from fellow students. Even experienced managers did not easily understand its propositions. This simple diagram was helpful for many:

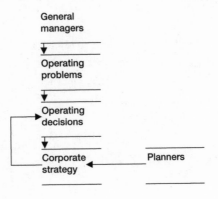

The illustration is of a general manager involved in operating problems and therefore in a position to influence operating decisions. Over time, a corporate strategy, apparent to the organization, evolves from the patterns discernible in operating decisions. At this point, the general manager insists that those who are making current operating decisions ensure that they are consistent with the corporate strategy.

Simultaneously, a planning department may be churning out statements on corporate strategy. The general manager insists that these planners' statements are also compatible with what he or she wants to do.

Given such circumstances, two further conclusions emerge:

- The company whose general manager is involved in operating decisions is more likely to have a creative corporate strategy than the company whose general manager relies on formal planning techniques. Formal planning tends to produce conventional, pedestrian strategies.
- The skills required for effective implementation of a strategy are in shorter supply than those needed for formal planning.

Bill, a former outstanding student who is now a senior general manager of a large company, recently talked to me about his experiences with management skills. Reflecting on his personal growth, Bill recalled that it took at least two years after he read the article before he began to understand it.

A new group of managers took over his company, then near collapse, and they struggled for several years to return the company to its former preeminence. During this period, Bill was in a position to observe closely all the changes made and he found that they affirmed the precepts outlined in the article. He saw for himself how top managers with the patience to search out "the corridors of comparative indifference," and to build unanimity in the organization, successfully proceeded with major new marketing plans, manufacturing processes, and product development. Their behavior was in sharp contrast with that of the earlier, unsuccessful managers who, in their desperation to turn the company around, tried to impose major strategic changes that the organization did not understand how to implement.

Putting Theory into Practice

The best way to learn the five skills I outlined in my article is to work with a general manager who exercises them. The experience will be much more effectual than enrolling in a strategy course or reading books and articles. For reasons I do not confess to understand, I have found women quicker to master the subtle shadings of meaning so critical to effective application of management techniques.

The evidence suggests that a general manager can transfer management skills from one company to another, and that failure to duplicate earlier successes in a new company or industry is likely traceable to a lack of marketing or technical knowledge. The mismatched "creative placements" that plague the upper levels of some American companies could only be conceived in the minds of executive searchers.

The good management precepts for business executives are applicable, moreover, with minor modifications, to general managers in nonbusiness settings. Former students who find themselves managing a government facility or a hospital or a college remind me regularly that they too rely on the five skills. A few months ago, the rector of St. Vincent de Paul Seminary in Boynton Beach, Florida invited me to volunteer my services to develop a course in parish management. Writing cases about the pastors of parishes has been a refreshing exposure to another important general management

area of our society. One pastor is adept at keeping informed; another is not. One saves himself for
the critical things; another tries to respond to every
demand. One is sensitive to the power structure;
another points to his authority. One provides a
good focus to parish activities; another is carried
along by the tide of events. One is alert for opportunities; another complains about not having
any. Familiar sounds from general managers in
business?

Twenty years is an ephemeral test of endurability
for a management philosophy. The rector of St. Vincent's loaned me a book on ancient Chinese phi-
losophers. Their aphorisms and parables, recorded
over two centuries ago, preserve counsels that are
still relevant for today's general managers.

Much has been learned about general management during the past two decades, but we are
still novices. As we try to learn more, we encounter
severe limitations in the attempt to expand our knowledge by interviews, questionnaires, and even case
writing. It's the unguarded moments when the general manager is not playing for the grandstand that
often reveal the most about his or her skills, attitudes,
and ways of thinking. Future probes of these deep
pockets of ignorance will surely bring enlightenments
that overshadow "present principles."

1. *Good General Managers Are Not Professional,* Selected Paper 53,
University of Chicago. Graduate School of Business. 1977.

Originally published in July–August 1984
Reprint 84416

New Templates for Today's Organizations

PETER F. DRUCKER

Executive Summary

TODAY'S BUSINESSES ARE increasingly complex
and diverse. In this article, a well-known organization theorist describes new principles of organization design now in use and their applications to
today's businesses and institutions. It is his position
that not only must the new principles make it possible for organizations to function and perform, but
they must also serve the higher goals of human
endeavor.

Mr. Drucker has contributed many articles
to HBR and has authored several books, including
The Effective Executive and *The Practice of Management*. The present article is a consolidation of
several chapters from his new book, *Management:
Tasks, Responsibilities, Practices*, published this

year by Harper & Row. Until 1972, Mr. Drucker
was professor of management at New York University. He is now Clarke Professor of Social Science
at Claremont Graduate School, Claremont,
California.

ORGANIZATION STRUCTURES ARE becoming
increasingly short-lived and unstable.

The "classical" organization structures of the 1920s
and 1930s, which still serve as textbook examples, stood
for decades without needing more than an occasional
touching up. American Telephone & Telegraph, General
Motors, DuPont, Unilever, and Sears, Roebuck main-
tained their organizational concepts, structures, and
basic components through several management genera-
tions and major changes in the size and scope of the
business. Today, however, a company no sooner finishes
a major job of reorganizing itself than it starts all over
again.

General Electric, for instance, finished a tremendous
organization overhaul around 1960, after almost a
decade of hard work; since then it has revamped both its
structure and its overall strategies at least twice. Similarly, Imperial Chemicals in Great Britain is restructuring
an organization design that is barely 10 years old. And
the same restlessness and instability afflict organization
structures and concepts in the large U.S. commercial
banks, in IBM, and in U.S. government agencies. For
instance, the Health, Education and Welfare Department
has been subjected to a "final" reorganization almost
every year in its 20-year history.

To some extent this instability is a result of gross overorganizing. Companies are resorting to reorganization as a kind of miracle drug in lieu of diagnosing their ailments. Every business observer can see dozens of cases where substantial, even massive organization surgery is being misapplied to take care of a fairly minor procedural problem, or—even more often—to avoid facing up to personnel decisions. Equally common is the misuse of reorganization as a substitute for hard thinking on objectives, strategies, and priorities. Few managers seem to recognize that the right organization structure is not performance itself, but rather a prerequisite of performance. The wrong structure is indeed a guarantee of nonperformance; it produces friction and frustration, puts the spotlight on the wrong issues, and makes mountains out of trivia. But "perfect organization" is like "perfect health": the test is the ills it does not have and therefore does not have to cure.

Even if unnecessary organization surgery were not as rampant in our institutions as unnecessary appendectomies, hysterectomies, and tonsillectomies are said to be in our hospitals, there would still be an organization crisis. Twenty years ago many managers had yet to learn that organization design and organization structure deserve attention, thinking, and hard work. Almost everyone accepts this today; indeed, organization studies have been one of the true "growth industries" of the past twenty years. But while a few years ago organization theory had "the answers," today all is confusion.

The crisis is simultaneously a crisis of organization theory and of organization practice. Ironically, what is happening is not at all what organization theorists like Chris Argyris, Warren Bennis, Douglas McGregor (and

I myself) have been predicting for at least 10 years: pressures for a more free-form and humanistic organization that provides greater scope for personal fulfillment play almost no part in the present organization crisis. Instead the main causes of instability are *changes in the objective task,* in the kind of business and institution to be organized. This is at the root of the crisis of organization practice.

The organization theorists' traditional answer to "organization crisis"—more organization development—is largely irrelevant to this new problem. Sometimes they seem to be pushing old remedies to cure a disease that no one has heard of before, and that inhabits a totally unfamiliar type of body. The kind of business and institution to be organized today is an enormously different beast from that of 20 years ago.

These changes in the objective task have generated new design principles that do not fit traditional organization concepts. And therein lies the crisis of theory. On the other hand, the past 20 years have also seen the emergence of new understandings of which organization needs require the most attention, and of how to go about the job of analyzing organization needs and designing organization structures. Only when we have an idea of what the new "body" looks like can we begin to treat its ills.

In what follows I compare old models with new realities and describe the new design principles. These principles can be matched to the tasks of modern management as well as to the formal needs of all organizations, independent of their purpose. In exploring these relationships, we can discern a way to avoid the organization crisis that affects so many businesses and institutions.

The Early Models

Twice in the short history of management we have had
the "final answer" to organization problems.

The first time was around 1910 when Henri Fayol, the
French industrialist, thought through what were, to him,
the universally valid functions of a manufacturing company. (I am using the word "function" in the common,
management sense, not in the way Fayol used it to
describe administrative concerns.) Of course, at that
time the manufacturing business presented the one truly
important organization problem.

Then in the early 1920s Alfred P. Sloan, Jr., in organizing General Motors, took the next step. He found "the
answer" for organizing a large, multidivisional manufacturing company. The Sloan approach built the individual
divisions on the functional structure that Fayol had
specified for a manufacturing business, that is, on engineering, manufacturing, selling, and so on; but it organized the business itself by the concept of federal
decentralization, that is, on the basis of decentralized
authority and centralized control. By the mid-1940s
GM's structure had become the model for larger organizations around the world.

Where they fit the realities that confront organization
designers and implementers today, the Fayol and Sloan
models are still unsurpassed. Fayol's functional organization is still the best way to structure a small business,
especially a small manufacturing business. Sloan's federal decentralization is still the best structure for the
big, single-product, single-market company like GM.
But more and more of the institutional reality that has
to be structured and organized does not "fit." Indeed the
very assumptions that underlay Sloan's work—and that

of Fayol—are not applicable to today's organization
challenges.

GM Model vs. Present Realities

There are at least six ways in which the GM structure no
longer serves as a model for present organization needs.

1. General Motors is a manufacturing business. Today
we face the challenge of organizing the large nonmanufacturing institution. There are not only the large financial businesses and the large retailers, but also, equally,
there are worldwide transportation, communications,
and customer service companies. The latter, while they
may manufacture a product, have their greatest emphasis on outside services (as most computer businesses do).
Then there are, of course, all the nonbusiness service
institutions, e.g., hospitals, universities, and government
agencies. These "nonmanufacturing" institutions are,
increasingly, the true center of gravity of any developed
economy. They employ the most people, and they both
contribute to and take the largest share of the gross
national product. They present the fundamental
organization problems today.

2. General Motors is essentially a single-product,
single-technology, single-market business. Even
accounting for the revenues of its large financial and
insurance subsidiaries, four fifths of its total revenue are
still produced by the automobile. Although Frigidaire
and Electromotive are large, important businesses and
leaders in the consumer appliance and locomotive
markets, respectively, they are but minor parts of GM.
Indeed, GM is unique among large companies in being
far less diversified today than it was 30 or 40 years ago.
Then, in the late 1930s and early 1940s, General Motors

had major investments in the chemical industry (Ethyl), in the aircraft industry (North American Aviation), and in earth-moving equipment (Euclid). All three are gone now and have not been replaced by new diversification activities outside the automotive field.

The cars that General Motors produces differ in details, such as size, horsepower, and price, but they are essentially one and the same product. A man who came up the line in, say, the Pontiac Division, will hardly find Chevrolet totally alien—and even Opel in Germany will not hold a great many surprises for him.

By contrast, the typical businesses of today are multi-product, multitechnology, and multimarket. They may not be conglomerates, but they are diversified. And their central problem is a problem General Motors did not have: the organization of complexity and diversity.

There is, moreover, an even more difficult situation to which the GM pattern cannot be applied: the large single-product, single-technology business that, unlike GM, cannot be subdivided into distinct and yet comparable parts. Typical are the "materials" businesses such as steel and aluminum companies. Here belong, also, the larger transportation businesses, such as railroads, airlines, and the large commercial banks. These businesses are too big for a functional structure; it ceases to be a skeleton and becomes a straitjacket. They are also incapable of being genuinely decentralized; no one part on its own is a genuine "business." Yet as we are shifting from mechanical to process technologies, and from making goods to producing knowledge and services, these large, complex, but integrated businesses are becoming more important than the multidivisional businesses of the 1920s and 1930s.

3. General Motors still sees its international operations as organizationally separate and outside. For

50 years it has been manufacturing and selling overseas, and something like one quarter of its sales are now outside North America. But in its organization structure, in its reporting relationships, and above all in its career ladders, GM is a U.S. company with foreign subsidiaries. Rather than leaning toward an international, let alone a multinational operation, GM's top management is primarily concerned with the U.S. market, the U.S. economy, the U.S. labor movement, the U.S. government, and so on. This traditional structure and viewpoint of GM's top management may, in large part, explain the substantial failure of GM to take advantage of the rapid expansion and growth of such major non-U.S. automobile markets as Europe, where GM's share has actually been dropping, or Brazil, where GM failed to anticipate a rapidly emerging automobile market.[1]

In contrast, during the last 20 years many other companies have become multinational. For these companies, a great many cultures, countries, markets, and governments are of equal, or at least of major, importance.

4. Because GM is a one-product, one-country company, information handling is not a major organization problem and thus not a major concern. At GM everyone speaks the same language, whether by that we mean the language of the automotive industry or American English. Everyone fully understands what the other one is doing or should be doing, if only because, in all likelihood, he has done a similar job himself. GM can, therefore, be organized according to the logic of the marketplace, and the logic of authority and decision. It need not, in its organization, concern itself a great deal with the logic and flow of information.

By contrast, multiproduct, multitechnology, and multinational companies have to design their organization structure to handle a large flow of information. At the very least they have to make sure that their organization structure does not violate the logic of information. And for this task, GM offers no guidance—GM did not have to tackle the problem.

5. Four out of every five GM employees are either manual production workers or clerks on routine tasks. In other words, GM employs yesterday's rather than today's labor force.

But the basic organization problem today concerns knowledge work and knowledge workers. They are the fastest growing element in every business; in service institutions, they are the core employees.

6. Finally, General Motors has been a "managerial" rather than an "entrepreneurial" business. The strength of the Sloan approach lay in its ability to manage, and manage superbly, what was already there and known.

Today's organizer is challenged by an increasing demand to organize entrepreneurship and innovation. But for this undertaking, the General Motors model offers no guidance.

New Design Principles

We do not know how to handle these new organization realities or how to satisfy their structural demands. Nevertheless, the organizing task has not waited. To tackle the new realities, we have in the past 20 years improvised ad hoc design solutions to supplement the Fayol and Sloan models. As a result, the organization architect now has available five so-called design principles, i.e., five distinct organization structures. The two traditional ones already mentioned have been known as principles of organization design for many years:

- Henri Fayol's functional structure.

- Alfred P. Sloan's federal decentralization.

Three are new; indeed they are so new that they are not generally known, let alone recognized, as design principles:

- Team organization.

- Simulated decentralization.

- Systems structure.

In team organization, a group—usually a fairly small one—is set up for a specific task rather than for a specific skill or stage in the work process. In the past 20 years we have learned that whereas team design was traditionally considered applicable only to short-lived, transitory, exceptional task-force assignments, it is equally applicable to some permanent needs, especially to the top-management and innovating tasks.

In an organization that is both too big to remain functionally organized and too integrated to be genuinely decentralized, simulated decentralization is often the organization answer. It sets up one function, one stage in the process, or one segment as if it were a distinct business with genuine profit and loss responsibility; it treats accounting fictions, transfer prices, and overhead allocations as if they were realities of the marketplace. For all its difficulties and frictions, simulated decentralization is probably the fastest growing organization design around these days. It is the only one that fits, albeit poorly, the materials, computer, chemical, and pharmaceutical companies, as well as the big banks; it is also the only design principle suited for the large university, hospital, or government agency.

Finally, in systems structure, team organization and simulated decentralization are combined. The prototype for this design principle was NASA's space program, in which a large number of autonomous units—large government bodies, individual research scientists, profit-seeking businesses, and large universities—worked together, organized and informed by the needs of the situation rather than by logic, and held together by a common goal and a joint top management. The large transnational company, which is a mix of many cultures, governments, businesses, and markets, is the present embodiment of an organization based on the systems concept.

None of the new design principles is easy or trouble-free. Compared to the traditional designs of functionalism and federal decentralization, they are indeed so difficult, complex, and vulnerable that many organization theorists maintain that they are not principles at all, but abominations.[2] And there is no question that wherever the traditional principles can be used, they should be; they are infinitely easier. The traditional principles are, however, far more limited in their scope than the new ones, and when misapplied they can cause even greater problems.

Design Logics

Each of the five design principles expresses or embodies a logic that makes that principle the appropriate one to apply when one or another task of management requires a structure. In this discussion we can identify three, or maybe four, logics upon which the five principles are based. For instance, although they do it differently, the functional and team design principles both embody *work* and *task* and are thus appropriate designs to consider when faced with work- or task-oriented management problems.

Historically these two design principles have been viewed as antithetical, but actually they are complementary. In the functionally organized structure, the work skills—manufacturing, accounting, and so on—are designed to be static; the work moves from one stage to others. In team structure, the work is conceived as static, with skills moving to meet the requirements of the task. Because of their complementary nature, these two design principles are the only possible choices for dealing with, say, the structure of knowledge. For if you need a specific task performed and a team effort would do it best, then you need static functions as bases from which persons, and their expertise, can be moved to form a team.

Two other design logics, corresponding to those involving work and task, can also be defined. Simulated decentralization and Sloan's federal decentralization both deal with *results* and *performance*. They are result-focused designs. Unlike functional and team structures, however, they are not complementary; they are not even alternatives. Federal decentralization is an "optimum," simulated decentralization a "lesser evil" to be resorted to only when the stringent requirements of federal decentralization cannot be met.

The last of the available design principles, systems design, is focused on *relationships,* another dimension of management. Because relations are inevitably both more numerous and less clearly definable than either work and task or results, a structure focused on relations will present greater difficulties than either a work-focused or a result-focused design. There are, however, organization problems, as in the true multinational business, in which the very complexity of relationships makes systems design the only appropriate design principle.

This rough classification indicates that at least one additional design principle might yet be developed. *Decision* is as much a dimension of management as are work and task, results and performance, and relations. Yet, so far, we know of no decision-focused design principle of organization structure, but should one ever be developed, it might have wide applicability.[3]

Ideally, an organization should be multiaxial, that is, structured around work and task, *and* results and performance, *and* relationships, *and* decisions. It would function as if it were a biological organism, like the human body with its skeleton and muscles, a number of nervous systems, and with circulatory, digestive, immunological, and respiratory systems, all autonomous yet interdependent. But in social structures we are still limited to designs that express only one primary dimension.

So, in designing organizations, we have to choose among different structures, each stressing a different dimension and each, therefore, with distinct costs, specific and fairly stringent requirements, and real limitations. There is no risk-free organization structure. And a design that is the best solution for one task may be only one of a number of equally poor alternatives for another task, and just plain wrong for yet a third kind of work.

Major Tasks of Management

A somewhat different way of viewing the relationships between the design logics and principles is to identify the principal tasks of management that the principles can structure. We have learned that, in a very general analysis, organization design should simultaneously structure and integrate three different kinds of work: (1) the operating task, which is responsible for producing the results of today's business; (2) the innovative task, which creates the company's tomorrow; and (3) the top-management task, which directs, gives vision, and sets the course for the business of both today and tomorrow. No one organization design is adequate to all three kinds of work; every business will need to use several design principles side-by-side.

In addition, each organization structure has certain formal specifications that have nothing to do with the purpose of the structure but are integral parts of the structure itself. Just as a human body can be described as having certain characteristics, regardless of the occupation of its inhabitant, so can an organization structure. Bodies have arms and legs, hands and feet, all related to each other; similarly, organizations are structured to satisfy the need for:

- *Clarity,* as opposed to simplicity. (The Gothic cathedral is not a simple design, but your position inside it is clear; you know where to stand and where to go. A modern office building is exceedingly simple in design, but it is very easy to get lost in one; it is not clear.)

- *Economy* of effort to maintain control and minimize friction.

- *Direction of vision* toward the product rather than the process, the result rather than the effort.

- *Understanding* by each individual of his own task as well as that of the organization as a whole.

- *Decision making* that focuses on the right issues, is action-oriented, and is carried out at the lowest possible level of management.

- *Stability,* as opposed to rigidity, to survive turmoil, and *adaptability* to learn from it.

- *Perpetuation and self-renewal,* which require that an organization be able to produce tomorow's leaders from within, helping each person develop continuously; the structure must also be open to new ideas.

Even though every institution, and especially every business, is structured in some way around all the dimensions of management, no one design principle is adequate to all their demands and needs. Nor does any one of the five available design principles adequately satisfy all of the formal specifications. The functional principle, for instance, has great clarity and high economy, and it makes it easy to understand one's own task. But even in the small business it tends to direct vision away from results and toward efforts, to obscure the organization's goals, and to sub-optimize decisions. It has high stability but little adaptability. It perpetuates and develops technical and functional skills, that is, middle managers, but it resists new ideas and inhibits top-management development and vision. And every one of the other four principles is similarly both a "good fit" against some formal organization specifications and a "misfit" against others.

One conclusion from this discussion is that organization structures can either be pure or effective, but they are unlikely to be both. Indeed, even the purest structure we know of, Alfred Sloan's GM, was actually mixed. It was not composed just of decentralized divisions, with functional organization within the divisions. It also contained, from the beginning, some sizable simulated decentralization. For instance, Fisher Body had responsibility for all body work but not for any final product.

And top management was clearly structured as a team, or rather as a number of interlocking teams.

This does not mean that an organization structure must by necessity be unwieldy or a confused mixture. The tremendous vitality of some older structures—Sears, Roebuck and GM, for instance—shows that a dynamic balance can be achieved. One implication is clear, however, and that is that pure structure *is* likely to end up badly botched. (This tendency may explain the difficulties that both GE and Imperial Chemicals—each trying for pure decentralization—have been experiencing.) Above all, our observations lead us to conclude that organization design is a series of risk-taking decisions rather than a search for the "one best way." And by and large, organization theorists and practitioners have yet to learn this.

Building the New Structure

There are a number of important lessons to be learned from the previous discussion and from the experiences of the past 20 years. Some concern new ideas or conclusions we have not recognized before, while others involve rethinking old concepts and relationships that we thought were settled years ago.

The first thing we can conclude is that Fayol and Sloan were right: good organization structures will not just evolve. The only things that evolve by themselves in an organization are disorder, friction, and malperformance. Nor is the right structure—or even the livable one—intuitive, any more than Greek temples or Gothic cathedrals were. Traditions may indicate where the problems and malfunctions are, but they are of little help in finding solutions. Organization design and structure require thinking, analysis, and a systematic approach.

Second, we have learned that designing an organization structure is not the first step, but the last. The first step is to identify and organize the building blocks of organization, that is, the key tasks that have to be encompassed in the final structure and that, in turn, carry the structural load of the final edifice. This is, of course, what Fayol did with his functions of a manufacturing company, when he designed them according to the work to be done.

We now know that building blocks are determined by the kind of contribution they make. And we know that the traditional classification of the contributions, e.g., the staff-and-line concept of conventional U.S. organization theory, is more of a hindrance to understanding than a help.

Designing the building blocks or tasks is, so to speak, the "engineering phase" of organization design. It provides the basic materials. And like all materials, these building blocks have their specific characteristics. They belong in different places and fit together in different ways.

We have also learned that "structure follows strategy." Organization is not mechanical. It is not done by assembly, nor can it be prefabricated. Organization is organic and unique to each individual business or institution. We realize now that structure is a means for attaining the objectives and goals of an institution. And if a structure is to be effective and sound, we must start with objectives and strategy.[4]

This is perhaps the most fruitful new insight we have in the field of organization. It may sound obvious, and it is. But some of the worst mistakes in organization building have been made by imposing on a living business a mechanistic model of an ideal organization.

Strategy—that is, the answer to the question: "What is our business? What should it be? What will it be ?"—determines the purpose of structure. It thereby determines the key tasks or activities in a given business or service institution. Effective structure is the design that makes these key activities function and produce results. In turn the key activities are the load-bearing elements of a functioning structure. Organization design is, or should be, primarily concerned with the key activities; other purposes are secondary.

Some of the new insights into organization design require us to unlearn old ideas. A few of the noisiest and most time-consuming battles in organization theory and practice are pure sham. They pose an either/or dichotomy when the correct answer is "both—in varying proportions."

The first of these sham battles that had better be forgotten is between task-focus and person-focus in job design and organization structure. Structure and job design have to be task-focused. But assignments have to fit both the person and the needs of the situation. There is no point in confusing the two, as the old and tiresome discussion of the nonproblem insists on doing. Work is always objective and impersonal; the job itself is always done by a person.

Somewhat connected with this old controversy is the discussion of hierarchical versus free-form organization.

Traditional organization theory knows only one kind of structure, applicable alike to building blocks and whole buildings. It is the so-called scalar organization, that is, the hierarchical pyramid of superior and subordinates.

Today another—equally doctrinaire—organization theory is becoming fashionable. It maintains that shape and structure are what we want them to be—they are, or should be, free form. Everything—shape, size, and apparently tasks—derive from interpersonal relations. Indeed, it is argued, the purpose of the structure is to make it possible for each person "to do his thing."

It is simply not true, however, that one of these forms represents total regimentation and the other total freedom. The amount of discipline required in both is the same; they only distribute it differently.

Hierarchy does not, as the critics allege, make the person at the top of the pyramid more powerful. On the contrary, the first effect of hierarchical organization is to protect the subordinate against arbitrary authority from above. A scalar or hierarchical organization does this by defining a sphere within which the subordinate has authority, a sphere within which the superior cannot interfere. It protects the subordinate by making it possible for him to say, "This is *my* assigned job." Protection of the subordinate also underlies the scalar principle's insistence that a man have only one superior. Otherwise, the subordinate is likely to find himself caught between conflicting demands, commands, interests, and loyalties. There is a lot of truth in the old proverb, "Better one bad master than two good ones."

At the same time, the hierarchical organization gives the most individual freedom. As long as the incumbent does whatever the assigned duties of his position are, he has done his job. He has no responsibility beyond it.

We hear a lot of talk these days about the individual's right to do his own thing. But the only organization structure in which this is remotely possible is a hierarchical one. It makes the least demands on the individual to subordinate himself to the goals of the organization or to gear his activities into the needs and demands of others.

Teams, by contrast, demand, above all, very great self-discipline from each member. Everybody has to do the team's "thing." Everybody has to take responsibility for the work of the entire team and for its performance. The one thing one cannot do on a team is one's own "thing."

Organization builders (and even organization theorists) will have to learn that sound organization structure needs both (a) a hierarchical structure of authority, and (b) a capacity to organize task forces, teams, and individuals for work on both a permanent and a temporary basis.

The 'One-way' Myth

Organization theory and organization practice still assume that there is "one final answer," at least for a particular business or institution. In itself, this belief is a large part of today's organization crisis. It leads to doctrinaire structures that impose one template on everybody and everything—e.g., operating and innovating components; manufacturing and service units; single-product and multimarket businesses. And if any person or process, no matter how insignificant, seems out of place, a total root-and-branch reorganization has to be done to accommodate it.

Maybe there is one right answer—but if so, we do not yet have it. Indeed for certain businesses and institutions, such as a large airline or government agency, we do not even have one poor answer—all we have are a multitude of equally unsatisfactory approaches. But, as remarked before, the organizing task will not wait; it will by necessity continue to be a central preoccupation of managers. Therefore, they had better learn to understand the design principles we already have. They must also learn the formal specifications of organization, and the relationships between the tasks of a business and the structures available to it.

The true lesson of the organization crisis is, however, quite different. It is that the traditional quest for the one right answer—a quest pursued as wholeheartedly by the new "heretics" of free-form organization as by the most orthodox classicists—pursues the wrong quarry. It misconceives an organization as something in itself rather than as a means to an end. But now we can see that liberation and mobilization of human energies—rather than symmetry, harmony, or consistency—are the purpose of organization. Human performance is both its goal and its test.

Notes

1. For a discussion of these developments, see the epilogue to the new edition of my *Concept of the Corporation* (New York, John Day, 1972).

2. This is, for instance, the verdict of organization theorist Harold Koontz, in his well-publicized article, "The Management Theory Jungle," *Journal of the Academy of Management*, December 1965; see also his "Making Sense of Management Theory," HBR, July–August 1962, p. 24.

3. Herbert A. Simon and his school have been attempting to develop one—at least this is how I read H.A. Simon's *Administrative Behavior* (New York, Macmillan, 1957) and I.G. March and H.A. Simon's *Organizations* (New York, John Wiley & Sons, 1958).

4. The fundamental work on this topic, an in-depth study
   of the design of modern organization in pioneering
   American companies such as DuPont, General Motors,
   and Sears, was done by Alfred D. Chandler in his book
   Strategy and Structure (Cambridge, M.I.T. Press, 1962).

Originally published in January–February 1974
Reprint 74102

How Competitive Forces Shape Strategy

MICHAEL E. PORTER

Executive Summary

THE NATURE AND degree of competition in an industry hinge on five forces: the threat of new entrants, the bargaining power of customers, the bargaining power of suppliers, the threat of substitute products or services (where applicable), and the jockeying among current contestants. To establish a strategic agenda for dealing with these contending currents and to grow despite them, a company must understand how they work in its industry and how they affect the company in its particular situation. The author details how these forces operate and suggests ways of adjusting to them, and, where possible, of taking advantage of them.

T HE ESSENCE OF STRATEGY formulation is coping
with competition. Yet it is easy to view competition too
narrowly and too pessimistically. While one sometimes
hears executives complaining to the contrary, intense
competition in an industry is neither coincidence nor
bad luck.

Moreover, in the fight for market share, competition
is not manifested only in the other players. Rather, competition in an industry is rooted in its underlying economics, and competitive forces exist that go well beyond
the established combatants in a particular industry.
Customers, suppliers, potential entrants, and substitute
products are all competitors that may be more or less
prominent or active depending on the industry.

The state of competition in an industry depends on
five basic forces, which are diagrammed in the exhibit on
page 65. The collective strength of these forces determines the ultimate profit potential of an industry. It
ranges from *intense* in industries like tires, metal cans,
and steel, where no company earns spectacular returns
on investment, to *mild* in industries like oil field services
and equipment, soft drinks, and toiletries, where there is
room for quite high returns.

In the economists' "perfectly competitive" industry,
jockeying for position is unbridled and entry to the
industry very easy. This kind of industry structure, of
course, offers the worst prospect for long-run profitability. The weaker the forces collectively, however, the
greater the opportunity for superior performance.

Whatever their collective strength, the corporate
strategist's goal is to find a position in the industry
where his or her company can best defend itself against
these forces or can influence them in its favor. The

collective strength of the forces may be painfully apparent to all the antagonists; but to cope with them, the strategist must delve below the surface and analyze the sources of each. For example, what makes the industry vulnerable to entry, What determines the bargaining power of suppliers?

Knowledge of these underlying sources of competitive pressure provides the groundwork for a strategic agenda of action. They highlight the critical strengths and weaknesses of the company, animate the positioning of the company in its industry, clarify the areas where strategic changes may yield the greatest payoff, and highlight the places where industry trends promise to hold the greatest significance as either opportunities or threats. Understanding these sources also proves to be of help in considering areas for diversification.

Contending Forces

The strongest competitive force or forces determine the profitability of an industry and so are of greatest importance in strategy formulation. For example, even a company with a strong position in an industry unthreatened by potential entrants will earn low returns if it faces a superior or a lower-cost substitute product—as the leading manufacturers of vacuum tubes and coffee percolators have learned to their sorrow. In such a situation, coping with the substitute product becomes the number one strategic priority.

Different forces take on prominence, of course, in shaping competition in each industry. In the ocean-going tanker industry the key force is probably the buyers (the major oil companies), while in tires it is powerful OEM buyers coupled with tough competitors. In the steel industry the key forces are foreign competitors and substitute materials.

Every industry has an underlying structure, or a set of fundamental economic and technical characteristics, that gives rise to these competitive forces. The strategist, wanting to position his or her company to cope best with its industry environment or to influence that environment in the company's favor, must learn what makes the environment tick.

This view of competition pertains equally to industries dealing in services and to those selling products. To avoid monotony in this article, I refer to both products and services as "products." The same general principles apply to all types of business.

A few characteristics are critical to the strength of each competitive force. I shall discuss them in this section.

THREAT OF ENTRY

New entrants to an industry bring new capacity, the desire to gain market share, and often substantial resources. Companies diversifying through acquisition into the industry from other markets often leverage their resources to cause a shake-up, as Philip Morris did with Miller beer.

The seriousness of the threat of entry depends on the barriers present and on the reaction from existing competitors that entrants can expect. If barriers to entry are high and newcomers can expect sharp retaliation from the entrenched competitors, obviously the newcomers will not pose a serious threat of entering.

There are six major sources of barriers to entry:

1. *Economies of scale*—These economies deter entry by forcing the aspirant either to come in on a large scale

or to accept a cost disadvantage. Scale economies in production, research, marketing, and service are probably the key barriers to entry in the mainframe computer industry, as Xerox and GE sadly discovered. Economies of scale can also act as hurdles in distribution, utilization of the sales force, financing, and nearly any other part of a business.

2. *Product differentiation*—Brand identification creates a barrier by forcing entrants to spend heavily to overcome customer loyalty. Advertising, customer service, being first in the industry, and product differences are among the factors fostering brand identification. It is perhaps the most important entry barrier in soft drinks, over-the-counter drugs, cosmetics, investment banking, and public accounting. To create high fences around their businesses, brewers couple brand identification with economies of scale in production, distribution, and marketing.

3. *Capital requirements*—The need to invest large financial resources in order to compete creates a barrier to entry, particularly if the capital is required for unrecoverable expenditures in up-front advertising or R&D. Capital is necessary not only for fixed facilities but also for customer credit, inventories, and absorbing start-up losses. While major corporations have the financial resources to invade almost any industry, the huge capital requirements in certain fields, such as computer manufacturing and mineral extraction, limit the pool of likely entrants.

4. *Cost disadvantages independent of size*—Entrenched companies may have cost advantages not available to potential rivals, no matter what their size and attainable economies of scale. These advantages can stem

from the effects of the learning curve (and of its first cousin, the experience curve), proprietary technology, access to the best raw materials sources, assets purchased at preinflation prices, government subsidies, or favorable locations. Sometimes cost advantages are legally enforceable, as they are through patents. (For an analysis of the much-discussed experience curve as a barrier to entry, see the insert at the end of this article.)

5. *Access to distribution channels*—The newcomer on the block must, of course, secure distribution of its product or service. A new food product, for example, must displace others from the supermarket shelf via price breaks, promotions, intense selling efforts, or some other means. The more limited the wholesale or retail channels are and the more that existing competitors have these tied up, obviously the tougher that entry into the industry will be. Sometimes this barrier is so high that, to surmount it, a new contestant must create its own distribution channels, as Timex did in the watch industry in the 1950s.

6. *Government policy*—The government can limit or even foreclose entry to industries with such controls as license requirements and limits on access to raw materials. Regulated industries like trucking, liquor retailing, and freight forwarding are noticeable examples; more subtle government restrictions operate in fields like ski-area development and coal mining. The government also can play a major indirect role by affecting entry barriers through controls such as air and water pollution standards and safety regulations.

The potential rival's expectations about the reaction of existing competitors also will influence its decision on whether to enter. The company is likely to have second thoughts if incumbents have previously lashed out at new entrants or if:

- The incumbents possess substantial resources to fight back, including excess cash and unused borrowing power, productive capacity, or clout with distribution channels and customers.

- The incumbents seem likely to cut prices because of a desire to keep market shares or because of industry-wide excess capacity.

- Industry growth is slow, affecting its ability to absorb the new arrival and probably causing the financial performance of all the parties involved to decline.

CHANGING CONDITIONS

From a strategic standpoint there are two important additional points to note about the threat of entry.

First, it changes, of course, as these conditions change. The expiration of Polaroid's basic patents on instant photography, for instance, greatly reduced its absolute cost entry barrier built by proprietary technology. It is not surprising that Kodak plunged into the market. Product differentiation in printing has all but disappeared. Conversely, in the auto industry economies of scale increased enormously with post-World War II automation and vertical integration—virtually stopping successful new entry.

Second, strategic decisions involving a large segment of an industry can have a major impact on the conditions determining the threat of entry. For example, the actions of many U.S. wine producers in the 1960s to step up product introductions, raise advertising levels, and expand distribution nationally surely strengthened the entry roadblocks by raising economies of scale and making access to distribution channels more difficult. Similarly, decisions by members of the recreational vehicle industry to vertically integrate in order to lower costs have greatly increased the economies of scale and raised the capital cost barriers.

POWERFUL SUPPLIERS AND BUYERS

Suppliers can exert bargaining power on participants in an industry by raising prices or reducing the quality of purchased goods and services. Powerful suppliers can thereby squeeze profitability out of an industry unable to recover cost increases in its own prices. By raising their prices, soft drink concentrate producers have contributed to the erosion of profitability of bottling companies because the bottlers, facing intense competition from powdered mixes, fruit drinks, and other beverages, have limited freedom to raise *their* prices accordingly. Customers likewise can force down prices, demand higher quality or more service, and play competitors off against each other—all at the expense of industry profits.

The power of each important supplier or buyer group depends on a number of characteristics of its market situation and on the relative importance of its sales or purchases to the industry compared with its overall business.

A *supplier* group is powerful if:

• It is dominated by a few companies and is more concentrated than the industry it sells to.

- Its product is unique or at least differentiated, or if it has built up switching costs. Switching costs are fixed costs buyers face in changing suppliers. These arise because, among other things, a buyer's product specifications tie it to particular suppliers, it has invested heavily in specialized ancillary equipment or in reaming how to operate a supplier's equipment (as in computer software), or its production lines are connected to the supplier's manufacturing facilities (as in some manufacture of beverage containers).

- It is not obliged to contend with other products for sale to the industry. For instance, the competition between the steel companies and the aluminum companies to sell to the can industry checks the power of each supplier.

- It poses a credible threat of integrating forward into the industry's business. This provides a check against the industry's ability to improve the terms on which it purchases.

- The industry is not an important customer of the supplier group. If the industry is an important customer, suppliers' fortunes will be closely tied to the industry, and they will want to protect the industry through reasonable pricing and assistance in activities like R&D and lobbying.

A *buyer* group is powerful if:

- It is concentrated or purchases in large volumes. Large volume buyers are particularly potent forces if heavy fixed costs characterize the industry—as they do in metal containers, corn refining, and bulk chemicals, for example—which raise the stakes to keep capacity filled.

- The products it purchases from the industry are standard or undifferentiated. The buyers, sure that they can always find alternative suppliers, may play one company against another, as they do in aluminum extrusion.

- The products it purchases from the industry form a component of its product and represent a significant fraction of its cost. The buyers are likely to shop for a favorable price and purchase selectively. Where the product sold by the industry in question is a small fraction of buyers' costs, buyers are usually much less price sensitive.

- It earns low profits, which create great incentive to lower its purchasing costs. Highly profitable buyers, however, are generally less price sensitive (that is, of course, if the item does not represent a large fraction of their costs).

- The industry's product is unimportant to the quality of the buyers' products or services. Where the quality of the buyers' products is very much affected by the industry's product, buyers are generally less price sensitive. Industries in which this situation obtains include oil field equipment, where a malfunction can lead to large losses, and enclosures for electronic medical and test instruments, where the quality of the enclosure can influence the user's impression about the quality of the equipment inside.

- The industry's product does not save the buyer money. Where the industry's product or service can pay for itself many times over, the buyer is rarely price sensitive; rather, he is interested in quality. This is true in services like investment banking and public accounting, where errors in judgment can be costly and embarrassing, and in businesses like the logging of oil wells, where an accurate survey can save thousands of dollars in drilling costs.

• The buyers pose a credible threat of integrating backward to make the industry's product. The Big Three auto producers and major buyers of cars have often used the threat of self-manufacture as a bargaining lever. But sometimes an industry engenders a threat to buyers that its members may integrate forward.

Most of these sources of buyer power can be attributed to consumers as a group as well as to industrial and

Forces Governing Competition in an Industry

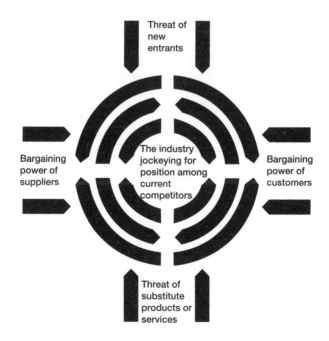

commercial buyers; only a modification of the frame of reference is necessary. Consumers tend to be more price sensitive if they are purchasing products that are undifferentiated, expensive relative to their incomes, and of a sort where quality is not particularly important.

The buying power of retailers is determined by the same rules, with one important addition. Retailers can gain significant bargaining power over manufacturers when they can influence consumers' purchasing decisions, as they do in audio components, jewelry, appliances, sporting goods, and other goods.

STRATEGIC ACTION

A company's choice of suppliers to buy from or buyer groups to sell to should be viewed as a crucial strategic decision. A company can improve its strategic posture by finding suppliers or buyers who possess the least power to influence it adversely.

Most common is the situation of a company being able to choose whom it will sell to—in other words, buyer selection. Rarely do all the buyer groups a company sells to enjoy equal power. Even if a company sells to a single industry, segments usually exist within that industry that exercise less power (and that are therefore less price sensitive) than others. For example, the replacement market for most products is less price sensitive than the overall market.

As a rule, a company can sell to powerful buyers and still come away with above-average profitability only if it is a low-cost producer in its industry or if its product enjoys some unusual, if not unique, features. In supplying large customers with electric motors, Emerson Electric earns high returns because its low cost position permits the company to meet or undercut competitors' prices.

If the company lacks a low cost position or a unique product, selling to everyone is self-defeating because the more sales it achieves, the more vulnerable it becomes. The company may have to muster the courage to turn away business and sell only to less potent customers.

Buyer selection has been a key to the success of National Can and Crown Cork & Seal. They focus on the segments of the can industry where they can create product differentiation, minimize the threat of backward integration, and otherwise mitigate the awesome power of their customers. Of course, some industries do not enjoy the luxury of selecting "good" buyers.

As the factors creating supplier and buyer power change with time or as a result of a company's strategic decisions, naturally the power of these groups rises or declines. In the ready-to-wear clothing industry, as the buyers (department stores and clothing stores) have become more concentrated and control has passed to large chains, the industry has come under increasing pressure and suffered falling margins. The industry has been unable to differentiate its product or engender switching costs that lock in its buyers enough to neutralize these trends.

SUBSTITUTE PRODUCTS

By placing a ceiling on prices it can charge, substitute products or services limit the potential of an industry. Unless it can upgrade the quality of the product or differentiate it somehow (as via marketing), the industry will suffer in earnings and possibly in growth.

Manifestly, the more attractive the price-performance trade-off offered by substitute products, the firmer the lid placed on the industry's profit potential. Sugar producers confronted with the large-scale commercialization of high-fructose corn syrup, a sugar substitute, are learning this lesson today.

Substitutes not only limit profits in normal times; they also reduce the bonanza an industry can reap in boom times. In 1978 the producers of fiberglass insulation enjoyed unprecedented demand as a result of high energy costs and severe winter weather. But the industry's ability to raise prices was tempered by the plethora of insulation substitutes, including cellulose, rock wool, and styrofoam. These substitutes are bound to become an even stronger force once the current round of plant additions by fiberglass insulation producers has boosted capacity enough to meet demand (and then some).

Substitute products that deserve the most attention strategically are those that (a) are subject to trends improving their price-performance trade-off with the industry's product, or (b) are produced by industries earning high profits. Substitutes often come rapidly into play if some development increases competition in their industries and causes price reduction or performance improvement.

JOCKEYING FOR POSITION

Rivalry among existing competitors takes the familiar form of jockeying for position—using tactics like price competition, product introduction, and advertising slugfests. Intense rivalry is related to the presence of a number of factors:

- Competitors are numerous or are roughly equal in size and power. In many U.S. industries in recent years foreign contenders, of course, have become part of the competitive picture.

- Industry growth is slow, precipitating fights for market share that involve expansion-minded members.

- The product or service lacks differentiation or switching costs, which lock in buyers and protect one combatant from raids on its customers by another.

- Fixed costs are high or the product is perishable, creating strong temptation to cut prices. Many basic materials businesses, like paper and aluminum, suffer from this problem when demand slackens.

- Capacity is normally augmented in large increments. Such additions, as in the chlorine and vinyl chloride businesses, disrupt the industry's supply-demand balance and often lead to periods of overcapacity and price cutting.

- Exit barriers are high. Exit barriers, like very specialized assets or management's loyalty to a particular business, keep companies competing even though they may be earning low or even negative returns on investment. Excess capacity remains functioning, and the profitability of the healthy competitors suffers as the sick ones hang on.[1] If the entire industry suffers from overcapacity, it may seek government help—particularly if foreign competition is present.

- The rivals are diverse in strategies, origins, and "personalities." They have different ideas about how to compete and continually run head-on into each other in the process.

As an industry matures, its growth rate changes, resulting in declining profits and (often) a shakeout. In the booming recreational vehicle industry of the early 1970s, nearly every producer did well; but slow growth since then has eliminated the high returns, except for the strongest members, not to mention many of the weaker companies. The same profit story has been played out in industry after industry—snowmobiles, aerosol packaging, and sports equipment are just a few examples.

An acquisition can introduce a very different personality to an industry, as has been the case with Black & Decker's takeover of McCullough, the producer of chain saws. Technological innovation can boost the level of fixed costs in the production process, as it did in the shift from batch to continuous-line photo finishing in the 1960s.

While a company must live with many of these factors—because they are built into industry economics— it may have some latitude for improving matters through strategic shifts. For example, it may try to raise buyers' switching costs or increase product differentiation. A focus on selling efforts in the fastest-growing segments of the industry or on market areas with the lowest fixed costs can reduce the impact of industry rivalry. If it is feasible, a company can try to avoid confrontation with competitors having high exit barriers and can thus sidestep involvement in bitter price cutting.

Formulation of Strategy

Once having assessed the forces affecting competition in an industry and their underlying causes, the corporate strategist can identify the company's strengths and weaknesses. The crucial strengths and weaknesses from a strategic standpoint are the company's posture vis-à-vis the underlying causes of each force. Where does it stand against substitutes? Against the sources of enery barriers?

Then the strategist can devise a plan of action that may include (1) positioning the company so that its capabilities provide the best defense against the competitive force; and/or (2) influencing the balance of the forces through strategic moves, thereby improving the company's position; and/or (3) anticipating shifts in the factors underlying the forces and responding to them, with the hope of exploiting change by choosing a strategy appropriate for the new competitive balance before opponents recognize it. I shall consider each strategic approach in turn.

POSITIONING THE COMPANY

The first approach takes the structure of the industry as given and matches the company's strengths and weaknesses to it. Strategy can be viewed as building defenses against the competitive forces or as finding positions in the industry where the forces are weakest.

Knowledge of the company's capabilities and of the causes of the competitive forces will highlight the areas where the company should confront competition and where avoid it. If the company is a low-cost producer, it may choose to confront powerful buyers while it takes care to sell them only products not vulnerable to competition from substitutes.

The success of Dr Pepper in the soft drink industry illustrates the coupling of realistic knowledge of corporate strengths with sound industry analysis to yield a superior strategy. Coca-Cola and PepsiCola dominate Dr Pepper's industry, where many small concentrate producers compete for a piece of the action. Dr Pepper chose a strategy of avoiding the largest-selling drink segment, maintaining a narrow flavor line, forgoing the development of a captive bottler network, and marketing heavily. The company positioned itself so as to be least vulnerable to its competitive forces while it exploited its small size.

In the $11.5 billion soft drink industry, barriers to entry in the form of brand identification, large-scale marketing, and access to a bottler network are enormous. Rather than accept the formidable costs and scale economies in having its own bottler network—that is, following the lead of the Big Two and of Seven-Up— Dr Pepper took advantage of the different flavor of its drink to "piggyback" on Coke and Pepsi bottlers who wanted a full line to sell to customers. Dr Pepper coped with the power of these buyers through extraordinary service and other efforts to distinguish its treatment of them from that of Coke and Pepsi.

Many small companies in the soft drink business offer cola drinks that thrust them into head-to-head competition against the majors. Dr Pepper, however, maximized product differentiation by maintaining a narrow line of beverages built around an unusual flavor.

Finally, Dr Pepper met Coke and Pepsi with an advertising onslaught emphasizing the alleged uniqueness of its single flavor. This campaign built strong brand identification and great customer loyalty. Helping its efforts was the fact that Dr Pepper's formula involved lower raw materials cost, which gave the company an absolute cost advantage over its major competitors.

There are no economies of scale in soft drink concentrate production, so Dr Pepper could prosper despite its small share of the business (6%). Thus Dr Pepper confronted competition in marketing but avoided it in product line and in distribution. This artful positioning combined with good implementation has led to an enviable record in earnings and in the stock market.

INFLUENCING THE BALANCE

When dealing with the forces that drive industry competition, a company can devise a strategy that takes the offensive. This posture is designed to do more than merely cope with the forces themselves; it is meant to alter their causes.

Innovations in marketing can raise brand identification or otherwise differentiate the product. Capital investments in large-scale facilities or vertical integration affect entry barriers. The balance of forces is partly a result of external factors and partly in the company's control.

EXPLOITING INDUSTRY CHANGE

Industry evolution is important strategically because evolution, of course, brings with it changes in the sources of competition I have identified. In the familiar product life-cycle pattern, for example, growth rates change, product differentiation is said to decline as the business becomes more mature, and the companies tend to integrate vertically.

These trends are not so important in themselves; what is critical is whether they affect the sources of competition. Consider vertical integration. In the maturing minicomputer industry, extensive vertical integration, both in manufacturing and in software development, is taking place. This very significant trend is greatly raising economies of scale as well as the amount of capital necessary to compete in the industry. This in turn is raising barriers to entry and may drive some smaller competitors out of the industry once growth levels off.

Obviously, the trends carrying the highest priority from a strategic standpoint are those that affect the most important sources of competition in the industry and those that elevate new causes to the forefront. In contract aerosol packaging, for example, the trend toward less product differentiation is now dominant. It has increased buyers' power, lowered the barriers to entry, and intensified competition.

The framework for analyzing competition that I have described can also be used to predict the eventual profitability of an industry. In long-range planning the task is to examine each competitive force, forecast the magnitude of each underlying cause, and then construct a composite picture of the likely profit potential of the industry.

The outcome of such an exercise may differ a great deal from the existing industry structure. Today, for example, the solar heating business is populated by dozens and perhaps hundreds of companies, none with a major market position. Entry is easy, and competitors are battling to establish solar heating as a superior substitute for conventional methods.

The potential of this industry will depend largely on the shape of future barriers to entry, the improvement of the industry's position relative to substitutes, the ultimate intensity of competition, and the power captured by buyers and suppliers. These characteristics will in turn be influenced by such factors as the establishment of brand identities, significant economies of scale or experience curves in equipment manufacture wrought by technological change, the ultimate capital costs to compete, and the extent of overhead in production facilities.

The framework for analyzing industry competition has direct benefits in setting diversification strategy. It provides a road map for answering the extremely difficult question inherent in diversification decisions: "What is the potential of this business?" Combining the framework with judgment in its application, a company may be able to spot an industry with a good future before this good future is reflected in the prices of acquisition candidates.

Multifaceted Rivalry

Corporate managers have directed a great deal of attention to defining their businesses as a crucial step in strategy formulation. Theodore Levitt, in his classic 1960 article in HBR, argued strongly for avoiding the myopia of narrow, product-oriented industry definition.[2] Numerous other authorities have also stressed the need to look beyond product to function in defining a business, beyond national boundaries to potential international competition, and beyond the ranks of one's competitors today to those that may become competitors tomorrow. As a result of these urgings, the proper definition of a company's industry or industries has become an endlessly debated subject.

One motive behind this debate is the desire to exploit new markets. Another, perhaps more important motive is the fear of overlooking latent sources of competition that someday may threaten the industry. Many managers concentrate so single-mindedly on their direct antagonists in the fight for market share that they fail to realize that they are also competing with their customers and their suppliers for bargaining power. Meanwhile, they also neglect to keep a wary eye out for new entrants to the contest or fail to recognize the subtle threat of substitute products.

The key to growth—even survival—is to stake out a position that is less vulnerable to attack from head-to-head opponents, whether established or new, and less vulnerable to erosion from the direction of buyers, suppliers, and substitute goods. Establishing such a position can take many forms—solidifying relationships with favorable customers, differentiating the product either substantively or psychologically through marketing, integrating forward or backward, establishing technological leadership.

Notes

1. For a more complete discussion of exit barriers and their implications for strategy, see my article, "Please Note Location of Nearest Exit," *California Management Review*, Winter 1976, p. 21.

2. Theodore Levitt, "Marketing Myopia," reprinted as an HBR Classic, September-October 1975, p. 26.

The Experience Curve as an Entry Barrier

IN RECENT YEARS, the experience curve has become widely discussed as a key element of industry structure. According to this concept, unit costs in many manufacturing industries (some dogmatic adherents say in *all* manufacturing industries) as well as in some service industries decline with "experience," or a particular company's cumulative volume of production. (The experience curve, which encompasses many factors, is a broader concept than the better known learning curve, which refers to the efficiency achieved over a period of time by workers through much repetition.)

The causes of the decline in unit costs are a combination of elements, including economies of scale, the learning curve for labor, and capital-labor substitution. The cost decline creates a barrier to entry because new competitors with no "experience" face higher costs than established ones, particularly the producer with the largest market share, and have difficulty catching up with the entrenched competitors.

Adherents of the experience curve concept stress the importance of achieving market leadership to maximize this barrier to entry, and they recommend aggressive action to achieve it, such as price cutting in anticipation of falling costs in order to build volume. For the combatant that cannot achieve a healthy market share, the prescription is usually, "Get out."

Is the experience curve an entry barrier on which strategies should be built? The answer is: not in every industry. In fact, in some industries, building a strategy on the experience curve can be potentially disastrous. That costs decline with experience in some industries is not news to corporate executives. The significance of the experience curve for strategy depends on what factors are causing the decline.

If costs are falling because a growing company can reap economies of scale through more efficient, automated facilities and vertical integration, then the cumulative volume of production is unimportant to its relative cost position. Here the lowest-cost producer is the one with the largest, most efficient facilities.

A new entrant may well be more efficient than the more experienced competitors; if it has built the newest plant, it will face no disadvantage in having to catch up. The strategic prescription, "You must have the largest, most efficient plant," is a lot different from, "You must produce the greatest cumulative output of the item to get your costs down."

Whether a drop in costs with cumulative (not absolute) volume erects an entry barrier also depends on the sources of the decline. If costs go down because of technical advances known generally in the industry or because of the development of improved equipment that can be copied or purchased from equipment suppliers, the experience curve is no entry barrier at all—in fact, new or less experienced competitors may actually enjoy a cost *advantage* over the leaders. Free of the legacy of heavy past investments, the newcomer or less experienced competitor can purchase or copy the newest and lowest-cost equipment and technology.

If, however, experience can be kept proprietary, the leaders will maintain a cost advantage. But new entrants may require less experience to reduce their costs than the leaders needed. All this suggests that the experience curve can be a shaky entry barrier on which to build a strategy.

While space does not permit a complete treatment here, I want to mention a few other crucial elements in determining the appropriateness of a strategy built on the entry barrier provided by the experience curve:

- The height of the barrier depends on how important costs are to competition compared with other areas like marketing, selling, and innovation.

- The barrier can be nullified by product or process innovations leading to a substantially new technology and thereby creating an entirely new experience curve.* New entrants can leapfrog the industry leaders and alight on the new experience curve, to which those leaders may be poorly positioned to jump.

- If more than one strong company is building its strategy on the experience curve, the consequences can be nearly fatal. By the time only one rival is left pursuing such a strategy, industry growth may have stopped and the prospects of reaping the spoils of victory long since evaporated.

*For an example drawn from the history of the automobile industry see William J. Abernathy and Kenneth Wayne, "The Limits of the Learning Curve," HBR September–October 1974, p. 109.

Originally published in March–April 1979
Reprint 79208

Power Failure in Management Circuits

ROSABETH MOSS KANTER

Executive Summary

WHEN ONE THINKS of "power," one often assumes that a person is the source of it and that some mystical charismatic element is at work. Of course, with some people this is undoubtedly so; they derive power from how other people perceive them. In organizations, however—says this author—power is not so much a question of people but of positions. Drawing a distinction between productive and oppressive power, the author maintains that the former is a function of having open channels to supplies, support, and information; the latter is a function of these channels being closed. She then describes three positions that are classically powerless: first-line supervisors, staff professionals, and, surprisingly, chief executive officers.

These positions can be powerless because of difficulties in maintaining open lines of information and
support. Seeing powerlessness in these positions as
dangerous for organizations, she urges managers
to restructure and redesign their organizations in
order to eliminate pockets of powerlessness.

POWER IS AMERICA'S LAST DIRTY word. It is
easier to talk about money—and much easier to talk
about sex—than it is to talk about power. People who
have it deny it; people who want it do not want to appear
to hunger for it; and people who engage in its machina-
tions do so secretly.

Yet, because it turns out to be a critical element in
effective managerial behavior, power should come out
from undercover. Having searched for years for those
styles or skills that would identify capable organization
leaders, many analysts, like myself, are rejecting individual traits or situational appropriateness as key and finding the sources of a leader's real power.

Access to resources and information and the ability to
act quickly make it possible to accomplish more and to
pass on more resources and information to subordinates.
For this reason, people tend to prefer bosses with "clout."
When employees perceive their manager as influential
upward and outward, their status is enhanced by association and they generally have high morale and feel less
critical or resistant to their boss.[1] More powerful leaders
are also more likely to delegate (they are too busy to do it
all themselves), to reward talent, and to build a team that
places subordinates in significant positions.

Powerlessness, in contrast, tends to breed bossiness rather than true leadership. In large organizations, at least, it is powerlessness that often creates ineffective, desultory management and petty, dictatorial, rules-minded managerial styles. Accountability without power—responsibility for results without the resources to get them—creates frustration and failure. People who see themselves as weak and powerless and find their subordinates resisting or discounting them tend to use more punishing forms of influence. If organizational power can "ennoble," then, recent research shows, organizational powerlessness can (with apologies to Lord Acton) "corrupt."[2]

So perhaps power, in the organization at least, does not deserve such a bad reputation. Rather than connoting only dominance, control, and oppression, *power* can mean efficacy and capacity—something managers and executives need to move the organization toward its goals. Power in organizations is analogous in simple terms to physical power: it is the ability to mobilize resources (human and material) to get things done. The true sign of power, then, is accomplishment—not fear, terror, or tyranny. Where the power is "on," the system can be productive; where the power is "off," the system bogs down.

But saying that people need power to be effective in organizations does not tell us where it comes from or why some people, in some jobs, systematically seem to have more of it than others. In this article I want to show that to discover the sources of productive power, we have to look not at the *person*—as conventional classifications of effective managers and employees do—but at the *position* the person occupies in the organization.

Where Does Power Come From?

The effectiveness that power brings evolves from two kinds of capacities: first, access to the resources, information, and support necessary to carry out a task; and, second, ability to get cooperation in doing what is necessary. (The first exhibit identifies some symbols of an individual manager's power.)

Both capacities derive not so much from a leader's style and skill as from his or her location in the formal and informal systems of the organization—in both job definition and connection to other important people in the company. Even the ability to get cooperation from subordinates is strongly defined by the manager's clout outward. People are more responsive to bosses who look as if they can get more for them from the organization.

We can regard the uniquely organizational sources of power as consisting of three "lines":

1. *Lines of supply.* Influence outward, over the environment, means that managers have the capacity to bring in the things that their own organizational

---

Some Common Symbols of a Manager's Organizational Power (Influence Upward and Outward)

To what extent a manager can—
  Intercede favorably on behalf of someone in trouble with the organization
  Get a desirable placement for a talented subordinate
  Get approval for expenditures beyond the budget
  Get above-average salary increases for subordinates
  Get items on the agenda at policy meetings
  Get fast access to top decision makers
  Get regular, frequent access to top decision makers
  Get early information about decisions and policy shifts

domain needs—materials, money, resources to
distribute as rewards, and perhaps even prestige.

2. *Lines of information.* To be effective, managers need
to be "in the know" in both the formal and the informal sense.

3. *Lines of support.* In a formal framework, a manager's
job parameters need to allow for non-ordinary
action, for a show of discretion or exercise of judgment. Thus managers need to know that they can
assume innovative, risk-taking activities without
having to go through the stifling multilayered
approval process. And, informally, managers need
the backing of other important figures in the organization whose tacit approval becomes another
resource they bring to their own work unit as well
as a sign of the manager's being "in."

Note that productive power has to do with *connections*
with other parts of a system. Such systemic aspects of
power derive from two sources—job activities and
political alliances:

1. Power is most easily accumulated when one has a job
that is designed and located to allow *discretion* (non-
routinized action permitting flexible, adaptive, and
creative contributions), *recognition* (visibility and
notice), and *relevance* (being central to pressing
organizational problems).

2. Power also comes when one has relatively close contact with *sponsors* (higher-level people who confer
approval, prestige, or backing), *peer networks* (circles
of acquaintanceship that provide reputation and
information, the grapevine often being faster than
formal communication channels), and *subordinates*

(who can be developed to relieve managers of some of their burdens and to represent the manager's point of view).

When managers are in powerful situations, it is easier for them to accomplish more. Because the tools are

Ways Organizational Factors Contribute to Power or Powerlessness

	Generates power when factor is	Generates powerlessness when factor is
Rules inherent in the job	few	many
Predecessors in the job	few	many
Established routines	few	many
Task variety	high	low
Rewards for reliability/ predictability	few	many
Rewards for unusual performance/innovation	many	few
Flexibility around use of people	high	low
Approvals needed for nonroutine decisions	few	many
Physical location	central	distant
Publicity about job activities	high	low
Relationship of tasks to current problem areas	central	peripheral
Focus of tasks	outside work unit	inside work unit
Interpersonal contact in the job	high	low
Contact with senior officials	high	low
Participation in programs, conferences, meetings	high	low
Participation in problem-solving task forces	high	low
Advancement prospects of subordinates	high	low

there, they are likely to be highly motivated and, in turn, to be able to motivate subordinates. Their activities are more likely to be on target and to net them successes. They can flexibly interpret or shape policy to meet the needs of particular areas, emergent situations, or sudden environmental shifts. They gain the respect and cooperation that attributed power brings. Subordinates' talents are resources rather than threats. And, because powerful managers have so many lines of connection and thus are oriented outward, they tend to let go of control downward, developing more independently functioning lieutenants.

The powerless live in a different world. Lacking the supplies, information, or support to make things happen easily, they may turn instead to the ultimate weapon of those who lack productive power—oppressive power: holding others back and punishing with whatever threats they can muster.

The second exhibit summarizes some of the major ways in which variables in the organization and in job design contribute to either power or powerlessness.

Positions of Powerlessness

Understanding what it takes to have power and recognizing the classic behavior of the powerless can immediately help managers make sense out of a number of familiar organizational problems that are usually attributed to inadequate people:

- The ineffectiveness of first-line supervisors.

- The petty interest protection and conservatism of staff professionals.

- The crises of leadership at the top.

Instead of blaming the individuals involved in organizational problems, let us look at the positions people occupy. Of course, power or powerlessness in a position may not be all of the problem. Sometimes incapable people *are* at fault and need to be retrained or replaced. (See the ruled insert, "Women Managers Experience Special Power Failures," for a discussion of another special case, women.) But where patterns emerge, where the troubles associated with some units persist, organizational power failures could be the reason. Then, as Volvo President Pehr Gyllenhammar concludes, we should treat the powerless not as "villains" causing headaches for everyone else but as "victims."[3]

FIRST-LINE SUPERVISORS

Because an employee's most important work relationship is with his or her supervisor, when many of them talk about "the company," they mean their immediate boss. Thus a supervisor's behavior is an important determinant of the average employee's relationship to work and is in itself a critical link in the production chain.

Yet I know of no U.S. corporate management entirely satisfied with the performance of its supervisors. Most see them as supervising too closely and not training their people. In one manufacturing company where direct laborers were asked on a survey how they learned their job, on a list of seven possibilities "from my supervisor" ranked next to last. (Only company training programs ranked worse.) Also, it is said that supervisors do not translate company policies into practice—for instance, that they do not carry out the right of every employee to frequent performance reviews or to career counseling.

In court cases charging race or sex discrimination,
first-line supervisors are frequently cited as the "discrim-
inating official."[4] And, in studies of innovative work
redesign and quality of work life projects, they often
appear as the implied villains; they are the ones who are
said to undermine the program or interfere with its
effectiveness. In short, they are often seen as "not sufficiently managerial."

The problem affects white-collar as well as blue-collar
supervisors. In one large government agency, supervisors
in field offices were seen as the source of problems con-
cerning morale and the flow of information to and from
headquarters. "Their attitudes are negative," said a
senior official. "They turn people against the agency; they
put down senior management. They build themselves up
by always complaining about headquarters, but prevent
their staff from getting any information directly. We
can't afford to have such attitudes communicated to
field staff."

Is the problem that supervisors need more management training programs or that incompetent people are
invariably attracted to the job? Neither explanation
suffices. A large part of the problem lies in the position
itself—one that almost universally creates powerlessness.

First-line supervisors are "people in the middle,"
and that has been seen as the source of many of their
problems.[5] But by recognizing that first-line supervisors
are caught between higher management and workers, we
only begin to skim the surface of the problem. There is
practically no other organizational category as subject to
powerlessness.

First, these supervisors may be at a virtual dead end in
their careers. Even in companies where the job used to
be a stepping stone to higher-level management jobs, it

is now common practice to bring in MBAs from the outside for those positions. Thus moving from the ranks of direct labor into supervision may mean, essentially, getting "stuck" rather than moving upward. Because employees do not perceive supervisors as eventually joining the leadership circles of the organization, they may see them as lacking the high-level contacts needed to have clout. Indeed, sometimes turnover among supervisors is so high that workers feel they can outwait—and outwit—any boss.

Second, although they lack clout, with little in the way of support from above, supervisors are forced to administer programs or explain policies that they have no hand in shaping. In one company, as part of a new personnel program supervisors were required to conduct counseling interviews with employees. But supervisors were not trained to do this and were given no incentives to get involved. Counseling was just another obligation. Then managers suddenly encouraged the workers to bypass their supervisors or to put pressure on them. The personnel staff brought them together and told them to demand such interviews as a basic right. If supervisors had not felt powerless before, they did after that squeeze from below, engineered from above.

The people they supervise can also make life hard for them in numerous ways. This often happens when a supervisor has himself or herself risen up from the ranks. Peers that have not made it are resentful or derisive of their former colleague, whom they now see as trying to lord it over them. Often it is easy for workers to break rules and let a lot of things slip.

Yet first-line supervisors are frequently judged according to rules and regulations while being limited by other regulations in what disciplinary actions they can take. They often lack the resources to influence or reward people; after all, workers are guaranteed their pay and benefits by someone other than their supervisors. Supervisors cannot easily control events; rather, they must react to them.

In one factory, for instance, supervisors complained that performance of their job was out of their control: they could fill production quotas only if they had the supplies, but they had no way to influence the people controlling supplies.

The lack of support for many first-line managers, particularly in large organizations, was made dramatically clear in another company. When asked if contact with executives higher in the organization who had the potential for offering support, information, and alliances diminished their own feelings of career vulnerability and the number of headaches they experienced on the job, supervisors in five out of seven work units responded positively. For them *contact* was indeed related to a greater feeling of acceptance at work and membership in the organization.

But in the two other work units where there was greater contact, people perceived more, not less, career vulnerability. Further investigation showed that supervisors in these business units got attention only when they were in trouble. Otherwise, no one bothered to talk to them. To these particular supervisors, hearing from a higher-level manager was a sign not of recognition or potential support but of danger.

It is not surprising, then, that supervisors frequently manifest symptoms of powerlessness: overly close supervision, rules-mindedness, and a tendency to do the job themselves rather than to train their people (since job skills may be one of the few remaining things they feel good about). Perhaps this is why they sometimes stand as roadblocks between their subordinates and the higher reaches of the company.

STAFF PROFESSIONALS

Also working under conditions that can lead to organizational powerlessness are the staff specialists. As advisers behind the scenes, staff people must sell their programs and bargain for resources, but unless they get themselves entrenched in organizational power networks, they have little in the way of favors to exchange. They are seen as useful adjuncts to the primary tasks of the organization but inessential in a day-to-day operating sense. This disenfranchisement occurs particularly when staff jobs consist of easily routinized administrative functions which are out of the mainstream of the currently relevant areas and involve little innovative decision making.

Furthermore, in some organizations, unless they have had previous line experience, staff people tend to be limited in the number of jobs into which they can move. Specialists' ladders are often very short, and professionals are just as likely to get "stuck" in such jobs as people are in less prestigious clerical or factory positions.

Staff people, unlike those who are being groomed for important line positions, may be hired because of a special expertise or particular background. But management rarely pays any attention to developing them into more general organizational resources. Lacking growth prospects themselves and working alone or in very small teams, they are not in a position to develop others or pass on power to them. They miss out on an important way that power can be accumulated.

Sometimes staff specialists, such as house counsel or organization development people, find their work being farmed out to consultants. Management considers them fine for the routine work, but the minute the activities involve risk or something problematic, they bring in outside experts. This treatment says something not only about their expertise but also about the status of their function. Since the company can always hire talent on a temporary basis, it is unclear that the management really needs to have or considers important its own staff for these functions.

And, because staff professionals are often seen as adjuncts to primary tasks, their effectiveness and therefore their contribution to the organization are often hard to measure. Thus visibility and recognition, as well as risk taking and relevance, may be denied to people in staff jobs.

Staff people tend to act out their powerlessness by becoming turf-minded. They create islands within the organization. They set themselves up as the only ones who can control professional standards and judge their own work. They create sometimes false distinctions between themselves as experts (no one else could possibly do what they do) and lay people, and this continues to keep them out of the mainstream.

One form such distinctions take is a combination of disdain when line managers attempt to act in areas the professionals think are their preserve and of subtle refusal to support the managers' efforts. Or staff groups battle with each other for control of new "problem areas," with the result that no one really handles the issue at all. To cope with their essential powerlessness, staff groups may try to elevate their own status and draw boundaries between themselves and others.

When staff jobs are treated as final resting places for people who have reached their level of competence in the organization—a good shelf on which to dump managers who are too old to go anywhere but too young to retire—then staff groups can also become pockets of conservatism, resistant to change. Their own exclusion from the risk-taking action may make them resist *anyone's* innovative proposals. In the past, personnel departments, for example, have sometimes been the last in their organization to know about innovations in human resource development or to be interested in applying them.

TOP EXECUTIVES

Despite the great resources and responsibilities concentrated at the top of an organization, leaders can be powerless for reasons that are not very different from those that affect staff and supervisors: lack of supplies, information, and support.

We have faith in leaders because of their ability to make things happen in the larger world, to create possibilities for everyone else, and to attract resources to the organization. These are their supplies. But influence outward—the source of much credibility downward—can diminish as environments change, setting terms and conditions out of the control of the leaders. Regardless of top management's grand plans for the organization, the environment presses. At the very least, things going on outside the organization can deflect a leader's attention and drain energy. And, more detrimental, decisions made elsewhere can have severe consequences for the organization and affect top management's sense of power and thus its operating style inside.

In the go-go years of the mid-1960s, for example, nearly every corporation officer or university president could look—and therefore feel—successful. Visible success gave leaders a great deal of credibility inside the organization, which in turn gave them the power to put new things in motion.

In the past few years, the environment has been strikingly different and the capacity of many organization leaders to do anything about it has been severely limited. New "players" have flexed their power muscles: the Arab oil bloc, government regulators, and congressional investigating committees. And managing economic decline is quite different from managing growth. It is no accident that when top leaders personally feel out of control, the control function in corporations grows.

As powerlessness in lower levels of organizations can manifest itself in overly routinized jobs where performance measures are oriented to rules and absence of change, so it can at upper levels as well. Routine work often drives out nonroutine work. Accomplishment becomes a question of nailing down details. Short-term results provide immediate gratifications and satisfy stockholders or other constituencies with limited interests.

It takes a powerful leader to be willing to risk short-term deprivations in order to bring about desired long-term outcomes. Much as first-line supervisors are tempted to focus on daily adherence to rules, leaders are tempted to focus on short-term fluctuations and lose sight of long-term objectives. The dynamics of such a situation are self-reinforcing. The more the long-term goals go unattended, the more a leader feels powerless and the greater the scramble to prove that he or she is in control of daily events at least. The more he is involved in the organization as a short-term Mr. Fix-it, the more out of control of long-term objectives he is, and the more ultimately powerless he is likely to be.

Credibility for top executives often comes from doing the extraordinary: exercising discretion, creating, inventing, planning, and acting in nonroutine ways. But since routine problems look easier and more manageable, require less change and consent on the part of anyone else, and lend themselves to instant solutions that can make any leader look good temporarily, leaders may avoid the risky by taking over what their subordinates should be doing. Ultimately, a leader may succeed in getting all the trivial problems dumped on his or her desk. This can establish expectations even for leaders attempting more challenging tasks. When Warren Bennis was president of the University of Cincinnati, a professor called him when the heat was down in a classroom. In writing about this incident, Bennis commented, "I suppose he expected me to grab a wrench and fix it."[6]

People at the top need to insulate themselves from the routine operations of the organization in order to develop and exercise power. But this very insulation can lead another source of powerlessness—lack of information. In one multinational corporation, top executives who are sealed off in a large, distant office, flattered and virtually babied by aides, are frustrated by their distance from the real action.[7]

At the top, the concern for secrecy and privacy is mixed with real loneliness. In one bank, organization members were so accustomed to never seeing the top leaders that when a new senior vice president went to the branch offices to look around, they had suspicion, even fear, about his intentions.

Thus leaders who are cut out of an organization's information networks understand neither what is really going on at lower levels nor that their own isolation may be having negative effects. All too often top executives design "beneficial" new employee programs or declare a new humanitarian policy (e.g., "Participatory management is now our style") only to find the policy ignored or mistrusted because it is perceived as coming from uncaring bosses.

The information gap has more serious consequences when executives are so insulated from the rest of the organization or from other decision makers that, as Nixon so dramatically did, they fail to see their own impending downfall. Such insulation is partly a matter of organizational position and, in some cases, of executive style.

For example, leaders may create closed inner circles consisting of "doppelgängers," people just like themselves, who are their principal sources of organizational information and tell them only what they want to know. The reasons for the distortions are varied: key aides want to relieve the leader of burdens, they think just like the leader, they want to protect their own positions of power, or the familiar "kill the messenger" syndrome makes people close to top executives reluctant to be the bearers of bad news.

Finally, just as supervisors and lower-level managers need their supporters in order to be and feel powerful, so do top executives. But for them sponsorship may not be so much a matter of individual endorsement as an issue of support by larger sources of legitimacy in the society. For top executives the problem is not to fit in among peers; rather, the question is whether the public at large and other organization members perceive a common interest which they see the executives as promoting.

If, however, public sources of support are withdrawn and leaders are open to public attack or if inside constituencies fragment and employees see their interests better aligned with pressure groups than with organizational leadership, then powerlessness begins to set in.

When common purpose is lost, the system's own politics may reduce the capacity of those at the top to act. Just as managing decline seems to create a much more passive and reactive stance than managing growth, so does mediating among conflicting interests. When what is happening outside and inside their organizations is out of their control, many people at the top turn into decline managers and dispute mediators. Neither is a particularly empowering role.

Thus when top executives lose their own lines of supply, lines of information, and lines of support, they too suffer from a kind of powerlessness. The temptation for them then is to pull in every shred of power they can and to decrease the power available to other people to act. Innovation loses out in favor of control. Limits rather than targets are set. Financial goals are met by reducing "overhead" (people) rather than by giving people the tools and discretion to increase their own productive capacity. Dictatorial statements come down from the top, spreading the mentality of powerlessness farther until the whole organization becomes sluggish and people concentrate on protecting what they have rather than on producing what they can.

When everyone is playing "king of the mountain," guarding his or her turf jealously, then king of the mountain becomes the only game in town.

To Expand Power, Share It

In no case am I saying that people in the three hierarchical levels described are always powerless, but they are susceptible to common conditions that can contribute to powerlessness. The third exhibit summarizes the most common symptoms of powerlessness for each level and some typical sources of that behavior.

I am also distinguishing the tremendous concentration of economic and political power in large corporations themselves from the powerlessness that can beset individuals even in the highest positions in such organizations. What grows with organizational position in hierarchical levels is not necessarily the power to accomplish—productive power—but the power to punish, to prevent, to sell off, to reduce, to fire, all without appropriate concern for consequences. It is that kind of power—oppressive power—that we often say corrupts.

The absence of ways to prevent individual and social harm causes the polity to feel it must surround people in power with constraints, regulations, and laws that limit the arbitrary use of their authority. But if oppressive power corrupts, then so does the absence of productive power. In large organizations, powerlessness can be a bigger problem than power.

David C. McClelland makes a similar distinction between oppressive and productive power:

"The negative . . . face of power is characterized by the dominance-submission mode: if I win, you lose. . . . It leads to simple and direct means of feeling powerful [such as being aggressive]. It does not often lead to effective social leadership for the reason that such a person tends to treat other people as pawns. People who feel they are pawns tend to be passive and useless to the

Common Symptoms and Sources of Powerlessness for Three Key Organizational Positions

Position	Symptoms	Sources
First-line supervisors	Close, rules-minded supervision	Routine, rules-minded jobs with little control over lines of supply
	Tendency to do things oneself, blocking of subordinates' development and information	Limited lines of information
	Resistant, underproducing subordinates	Limited advancement or involvement prospects for oneself/subordinates
Staff professionals	Turf protection, information control	Routine tasks seen as peripheral to "real tasks" of line organization
	Retreat into professionalism	Blocked careers
	Conservative resistance to change	Easy replacement by outside experts
Top executives	Focus on internal cutting, short-term results, "punishing"	Uncontrollable lines of supply because of environmental changes
	Dictatorial top-down communications	Limited or blocked lines of information about lower levels of organization
	Retreat to comfort of like-minded lieutenants	Diminished lines of support because of challenges to legitimacy (e.g., from the public or special interest groups)

leader who gets his satisfaction from dominating them. Slaves are the most inefficient form of labor ever devised by man. If a leader wants to have far-reaching influence, he must make his followers feel powerful and able to accomplish things on their own. . . . Even the most dictatorial leader does not succeed if he has not instilled in at least some of his followers a sense of power and the strength to pursue the goals he has set."[8]

Organizational power can grow, in part, by being shared. We do not yet know enough about new organizational forms to say whether productive power is infinitely expandable or where we reach the point of diminishing returns. But we do know that sharing power is different from giving or throwing it away. Delegation does not mean abdication.

Some basic lessons could be translated from the field of economics to the realm of organizations and management. Capital investment in plants and equipment is not the only key to productivity. The productive capacity of nations, like organizations, grows if the skill base is upgraded. People with the tools, information, and support to make more informed decisions and act more quickly can often accomplish more. By empowering others, a leader does not decrease his power; instead he may increase it—especially if the whole organization performs better.

This analysis leads to some counterintuitive conclusions. In a certain tautological sense, the principal problem of the powerless is that they lack power. Powerless people are usually the last ones to whom anyone wants to entrust more power, for fear of its dissipation or abuse. But those people are precisely the ones who might benefit most from an injection of power and whose behavior is likely to change as new options open up to them.

Also, if the powerless bosses could be encouraged to share some of the power they do have, their power would grow. Yet, of course, only those leaders who feel secure about their own power outward—their lines of supply, information, and support—can see empowering subordinates as a gain rather than a loss. The two sides of power (getting it and giving it) are closely connected.

There are important lessons here for both subordinates and those who want to change organizations, whether executives or change agents. Instead of resisting or criticizing a powerless boss, which only increases the boss's feeling of powerlessness and need to control, subordinates instead might concentrate on helping the boss become more powerful. Managers might make pockets of ineffectiveness in the organization more productive not by training or replacing individuals but by structural solutions such as opening supply and support lines.

Similarly, organizational change agents who want a new program or policy to succeed should make sure that the change itself does not render any other level of the organization powerless. In making changes, it is wise to make sure that the key people in the level or two directly above and in neighboring functions are sufficiently involved, informed, and taken into account, so that the program can be used to build their own sense of power also. If such involvement is impossible, then it is better to move these people out of the territory altogether than to leave behind a group from whom some power has been removed and who might resist and undercut the program.

In part, of course, spreading power means educating people to this new definition of it. But words alone will not make the difference; managers will need the real experience of a new way of managing.

Here is how the associate director of a large corporate professional department phrased the lessons that he learned in the transition to a team-oriented, participatory, power-sharing management process:

"Get in the habit of involving your own managers in decision making and approvals. But don't abdicate! Tell them what you want and where you're coming from. Don't go for a one-boss grassroots 'democracy.' Make the management hierarchy work for you in participation . . .

"Hang in there, baby, and don't give up. Try not to 'revert' just because everything seems to go sour on a particular day. Open up—talk to people and tell them how you feel. They'll want to get you back on track and will do things to make that happen—because they don't really want to go back to the way it was. . . . Subordinates will push you to 'act more like a boss,' but their interest is usually more in seeing someone else brought to heel than getting bossed themselves."

Naturally, people need to have power before they can learn to share it. Exhorting managers to change their leadership styles is rarely useful by itself. In one large plant of a major electronics company, first-line production supervisors were the source of numerous complaints from managers who saw them as major roadblocks to overall plant productivity and as insufficiently skilled supervisors. So the plant personnel staff undertook two pilot programs to increase the supervisors' effectiveness. The first program was based on a traditional competency and training model aimed at teaching the specific skills of successful supervisors. The second program, in contrast, was designed to empower the supervisors by directly affecting their flexibility, access to resources, connections with higher-level officials, and control over working conditions.

After an initial gathering of data from supervisors and their subordinates, the personnel staff held meetings where all the supervisors were given tools for developing action plans for sharing the data with their people and collaborating on solutions to perceived problems. But then, in a departure from common practice in this organization, task forces of supervisors were formed to develop new systems for handling job and career issues common to them and their people. These task forces were given budgets, consultants, representation on a plantwide project steering committee alongside managers at much higher levels, and wide latitude in defining the nature and scope of the changes they wished to make. In short, lines of supply, information, and support were opened to them.

As the task forces progressed in their activities, it became clear to the plant management that the hoped-for changes in supervisory effectiveness were taking place much more rapidly through these structural changes in power than through conventional management training; so the conventional training was dropped. Not only did the pilot groups design useful new procedures for the plant, astonishing senior management in several cases with their knowledge and capabilities, but also, significantly, they learned to manage their own people better.

Several groups decided to involve shop-floor workers in their task forces; they could now see from their own experience the benefits of involving subordinates in solving job-related problems. Other supervisors began to experiment with ways to implement "participatory management" by giving subordinates more control and influence without relinquishing their own authority.

Soon the "problem supervisors" in the "most troubled plant in the company" were getting the highest possible performance ratings and were considered models for direct production management. The sharing of organizational power from the top made possible the productive use of power below.

One might wonder why more organizations do not adopt such empowering strategies. There are standard answers: that giving up control is threatening to people who have fought for every shred of it; that people do not want to share power with those they look down on; that managers fear losing their own place and special privileges in the system; that "predictability" often rates higher than "flexibility" as an organizational value; and so forth.

But I would also put skepticism about employee abilities high on the list. Many modern bureaucratic systems are designed to minimize dependence on individual intelligence by making routine as many decisions as possible. So it often comes as a genuine surprise to top executives that people doing the more routine jobs could, indeed, make sophisticated decisions or use resources entrusted to them in intelligent ways.

In the same electronics company just mentioned, at the end of a quarter the pilot supervisory task forces were asked to report results and plans to senior management in order to have their new budget requests approved. The task forces made sure they were well prepared, and the high-level executives were duly impressed. In fact, they were *so* impressed that they kept interrupting the presentations with compliments, remarking that the supervisors could easily be doing sophisticated personnel work.

At first the supervisors were flattered. Such praise from upper management could only be taken well. But when the first glow wore off, several of them became very angry. They saw the excessive praise as patronizing and insulting. "Didn't they think we could think? Didn't they imagine we were capable of doing this kind of work?" one asked. "They must have seen us as just a bunch of animals. No wonder they gave us such limited jobs."

As far as these supervisors were concerned, their abilities had always been there, in latent form perhaps, but still there. They as individuals had not changed—just their organizational power.

Women Managers Experience Special Power Failures

THE TRADITIONAL problems of women in management are illustrative of how formal and informal practices can combine to engender powerlessness. Historically, women in management have found their opportunities in more routine, low-profile jobs. In staff positions, where they serve in support capacities to line managers but have no line responsibilities of their own, or in supervisory jobs managing "stuck" subordinates, they are not in a position either to take the kinds of risks that build credibility or to develop their own team by pushing bright subordinates.

Such jobs, which have few favors to trade, tend to keep women out of the mainstream of the organization. This lack of clout, coupled with the greater difficulty anyone who is "different" has in getting into the information and support networks, has meant that merely by organizational situation women in management have been more likely than men to be rendered structurally powerless. This is one reason those women who have achieved power have often had family connections that put them in the mainstream of the organization's social circles.

A disproportionate number of women managers are found among first-line supervisors or staff professionals; and they, like men in those circumstances, are likely to be organizationally powerless. But the behavior of other managers can contribute to the powerlessness of women in management in a number of less obvious ways.

One way other managers can make a woman powerless is by patronizingly overprotecting her: putting her in "a safe job," not giving her enough to do to prove herself, and not suggesting her for high-risk, visible assignments. This protectiveness is sometimes born of "good" intentions to give her every chance to succeed (why stack the deck against her?). Out of managerial concerns, out of awareness that a woman may be up against situations that men simply do not have to face, some very well-meaning managers protect their female managers ("It's a jungle, so why send her into it?").

Overprotectiveness can also mask a manager's fear of association with a woman should she fail. One senior bank official at a level below vice president told me about his concerns with respect to a

high-performing, financially experienced woman
reporting to him. Despite *his* overwhelmingly positive work experiences with her, he was still afraid
to recommend her for other assignments because
he felt it was a personal risk. "What if other managers are not as accepting of women as I am?" he
asked. "I know I'd be sticking my neck out; they
would take her more because of my endorsement
than her qualifications. And what if she doesn't
make it? My judgment will be on the line."

Overprotection is relatively benign compared
with rendering a person powerless by providing
obvious signs of lack of managerial support. For
example, allowing someone supposedly in authority to be bypassed easily means that no one else
has to take him or her seriously. If a woman's
immediate supervisor or other managers listen willingly to criticism of her and show they are concerned every time a negative comment comes up
and that they assume she must be at fault, then they
are helping to undercut her. If managers let other
people know that they have concerns about this
person or that they are testing her to see how she
does, then they are inviting other people to look for
signs of inadequacy or failure.

Furthermore, people assume they can afford to
bypass women because they "must be uninformed"
or "don't know the ropes." Even though women
may be respected for their competence or expertise, they are not necessarily seen as being
informed beyond the technical requirements of the
job. There may be a grain of historical truth in this.
Many women come to senior management posi-

tions as "outsiders" rather than up through the usual channels.

Also, because until very recently men have not felt comfortable seeing women as businesspeople (business clubs have traditionally excluded women), they have tended to seek each other out for informal socializing. Anyone, male or female, seen as organizationally naive and lacking sources of "inside dope" will find his or her own lines of information limited.

Finally, even when women are able to achieve some power on their own, they have not necessarily been able to translate such personal credibility into an organizational power base. To create a network of supporters out of individual clout requires that a person pass on and share power, that subordinates and peers be empowered by virtue of their connection with that person. Traditionally, neither men nor women have seen women as capable of sponsoring others, even though they may be capable of achieving and succeeding on their own. Women have been viewed as the *recipients* of sponsorship rather than as the sponsors themselves.

(As more women prove themselves in organizations and think more self-consciously about bringing along young people, this situation may change. However, I still hear many more questions from women managers about how they can benefit from mentors, sponsors, or peer networks than about how they themselves can start to pass on favors and make use of their own resources to benefit others.)

Viewing managers in terms of power and powerlessness helps explain two familiar stereotypes about women and leadership in organizations: that no one wants a woman boss (although studies show that anyone who has ever had a woman boss is likely to have had a positive experience), and that the reason no one wants a woman boss is that women are "too controlling, rules-minded, and petty."

The first stereotype simply makes clear that power is important to leadership. Underneath the preference for men is the assumption that, given the current distribution of people in organizational leadership positions, men are more likely than women to be in positions to achieve power and, therefore, to share their power with others. Similarly, the "bossy woman boss" stereotype is a perfect picture of powerlessness. All of these traits are just as characteristic of men who are powerless, but women are slightly more likely, because of circumstances I have mentioned, to find themselves powerless than are men. Women with power in the organization are just as effective—and preferred—as men.

Recent interviews conducted with about 600 bank managers show that, when a woman exhibits the petty traits of powerlessness, people assume that she does so "because she is a woman." A striking difference is that, when a man engages in the same behavior, people assume the behavior is a matter of his own individual style and characteristics and do not conclude that it reflects on the suitability of men for management.

Notes

1. Donald C. Pelz, "Influence: A Key to Effective Leadership in the First-Line Supervisor," *Personnel,* November 1952, p. 209.

2. See my book, *Men and Women of the Corporation* (New York: Basic Books, 1977), pp. 164–205; and David Kipnis, *The Powerholders* (Chicago: University of Chicago Press, 1976).

3. Pehr G. Gyllenhammar, *People at Work* (Reading, Mass.: Addison-Wesley, 1977), p. 133.

4. William E. Fulmer, "Supervisory Selection: The Acid Test of Affirmative Action," *Personnel,* November–December 1976, p. 40.

5. See my chapter (coauthor, Barry A. Stein), "Life in the Middle: Getting In, Getting Up, and Getting Along," in *Life in Organizations,* eds. Rosabeth M. Kanter and Barry A. Stein (New York: Basic Books, 1979).

6. Warren Bennis, *The Unconscious Conspiracy: Why Leaders Can't Lead* (New York: AMACOM, 1976).

7. See my chapter, "How the Top is Different," in *Life in Organizations.*

8. David C. McClelland, *Power: The Inner Experience* (New York: Irvington Publishers, 1975), p. 263. Quoted by permission.

Originally published in July–August 1979
Reprint 79403

Managing Your Boss

JOHN J. GABARRO AND JOHN P. KOTTER

Executive Summary

"WHEN WE FIRST wrote this article late in 1979, the idea of managing your boss was an illegitimate notion," recalls author John Gabarro. "Except for one article that Peter Drucker had written about 20 years earlier, there was nothing in management literature on the idea."

At the time, Gabarro and coauthor John Kotter were working together on organizational behavior at Harvard Business School. Doing very different kinds of field research on effective managers, both found that managing one's own boss was crucial to success. In fact, effective managers handled lateral, upward, and downward relationships equally well.

As Gabarro and Kotter developed more data, the value of boss-managing became more and more clear to them. Their focus on what works, or effective behavior, led them to an insight that still cuts through the folklore. Forget ambition. Forget promotion. Forget raises. Just think of the job and how to be effective in it. How do you get the resources you need—the information, the advice, even the permission? The answers always point toward whoever has the power, the leverage, that is, the boss. To fail to make that relationship one of mutual respect and understanding is to miss a major factor of effectiveness.

When they realized they were on to something basic, Gabarro and Kotter took their notes to an HBR editor, who immediately agreed to work with them on this landmark article. Published 13 years ago in January–February 1980, "Managing Your Boss" is one of HBR's best-selling reprints.

To MANY PEOPLE, THE PHRASE "managing your boss" may sound unusual or suspicious. Because of the traditional top-down emphasis in most organizations, it is not obvious why you need to manage relationships upward—unless, of course, you would do so for personal or political reasons. But we are not referring to political maneuvering or to apple polishing. We are using the term to mean the process of consciously working with your superior to obtain the best possible results for you, your boss, and the company.

Recent studies suggest that effective managers take time and effort to manage not only relationships with their subordinates but also those with their bosses.

These studies also show that this essential aspect of management is sometimes ignored by otherwise talented and aggressive managers. Indeed, some managers who actively and effectively supervise subordinates, products, markets, and technologies assume an almost passively reactive stance vis-à-vis their bosses. Such a stance almost always hurts them and their companies.

If you doubt the importance of managing your relationship with your boss or how difficult it is to do so effectively, consider for a moment the following sad but telling story.

Frank Gibbons was an acknowledged manufacturing genius in his industry and, by any profitability standard, a very effective executive. In 1973, his strengths propelled him into the position of vice president of manufacturing for the second largest and most profitable company in its industry. Gibbons was not, however, a good manager of people. He knew this, as did others in his company and his industry. Recognizing this weakness, the president made sure that those who reported to Gibbons were good at working with people and could compensate for his limitations. The arrangement worked well.

In 1975, Philip Bonnevie was promoted into a position reporting to Gibbons. In keeping with the previous pattern, the president selected Bonnevie because he had an excellent track record and a reputation for being good with people. In making that selection, however, the president neglected to notice that, in his rapid rise through the organization, Bonnevie had always had good-to-excellent bosses. He had never been forced to manage a relationship with a difficult boss. In retrospect, Bonnevie admits he had never thought that managing his boss was a part of his job.

Fourteen months after he started working for Gibbons, Bonnevie was fired. During that same quarter, the company reported a net loss for the first time in seven years. Many of those who were close to these events say that they don't really understand what happened. This much is known, however: While the company was bringing out a major new product—a process that required sales, engineering, and manufacturing groups to coordinate decisions very carefully—a whole series of misunderstandings and bad feelings developed between Gibbons and Bonnevie.

For example, Bonnevie claims Gibbons was aware of and had accepted Bonnevie's decision to use a new type of machinery to make the new product; Gibbons swears he did not. Furthermore, Gibbons claims he made it clear to Bonnevie that the introduction of the product was too important to the company in the short run to take any major risks.

As a result of such misunderstandings, planning went awry: A new manufacturing plant was built that could not produce the new product designed by engineering, in the volume desired by sales, at a cost agreed on by the executive committee. Gibbons blamed Bonnevie for the mistake. Bonnevie blamed Gibbons.

Of course, one could argue that the problem here was caused by Gibbons's inability to manage his subordinates. But one can make just as strong a case that the problem was related to Bonnevie's inability to manage his boss. Remember, Gibbons was not having difficulty with any other subordinates. Moreover, given the personal price paid by Bonnevie (being fired and having his reputation within the industry severely tarnished), there was little consolation in saying the problem was that Gibbons was poor at managing subordinates. Everyone already knew that.

We believe that the situation could have turned out differently had Bonnevie been more adept at understanding Gibbons and at managing his relationship with him. In this case, an inability to manage upward was unusually costly. The company lost $2 million to $5 million, and Bonnevie's career was, at least temporarily, disrupted. Many less costly cases similar to this probably occur regularly in all major corporations, and the cumulative effect can be very destructive.

Misreading the Boss–Subordinate Relationship

People often dismiss stories like the one we just related as being merely cases of personality conflict. Because two people can on occasion be psychologically or temperamentally incapable of working together, this can be an apt description. But more often, we have found, a personality conflict is only a part of the problem— sometimes a very small part.

Bonnevie did not just have a different personality from Gibbons, he also made or had unrealistic assumptions and expectations about the very nature of boss–subordinate relationships. Specifically, he did not recognize that his relationship to Gibbons involved *mutual dependence* between two *fallible* human beings. Failing to recognize this, a manager typically either avoids trying to manage his or her relationship with a boss or manages it ineffectively.

Some people behave as if their bosses were not very dependent on them. They fail to see how much the boss needs their help and cooperation to do his or her job effectively. These people refuse to acknowledge that the boss can be severely hurt by their actions and needs cooperation, dependability, and honesty from them.

Some people see themselves as not very dependent on their bosses. They gloss over how much help and information they need from the boss in order to perform their own jobs well. This superficial view is particularly damaging when a manager's job and decisions affect other parts of the organization, as was the case in Bonnevie's situation. A manager's immediate boss can play a critical role in linking the manager to the rest of the organization, making sure the manager's priorities are consistent with organizational needs, and in securing the resources the manager needs to perform well. Yet some managers need to see themselves as practically self-sufficient, as not needing the critical information and resources a boss can supply.

Many managers, like Bonnevie, assume that the boss will magically know what information or help their subordinates need and provide it to them. Certainly, some bosses do an excellent job of caring for their subordinates in this way, but for a manager to expect that from all bosses is dangerously unrealistic. A more reasonable expectation for managers to have is that modest help will be forthcoming. After all, bosses are only human. Most really effective managers accept this fact and assume primary responsibility for their own careers and development. They make a point of seeking the information and help they need to do a job instead of waiting for their bosses to provide it.

In light of the foregoing, it seems to us that managing a situation of mutual dependence among fallible human beings requires the following:

1. You have a good understanding of the other person and yourself, especially regarding strengths, weaknesses, work styles, and needs.

2. You use this information to develop and manage a healthy working relationship—one that is compatible with both people's work styles and assets, is characterized by mutual expectations, and meets the most critical needs of the other person.

This combination is essentially what we have found highly effective managers doing.

Understanding the Boss

Managing your boss requires that you gain an understanding of the boss and his or her context, as well as your own situation. All managers do this to some degree, but many are not thorough enough.

At a minimum, you need to appreciate your boss's goals and pressures, his or her strengths and weaknesses. What are your boss's organizational and personal objectives, and what are his or her pressures, especially those from his or her own boss and others at the same level? What are your boss's long suits and blind spots? What is the preferred style of working? Does your boss like to get information through memos, formal meetings, or phone calls? Does he or she thrive on conflict or try to minimize it? Without this information, a manager is flying blind when dealing with the boss, and unnecessary conflicts, misunderstandings, and problems are inevitable.

In one situation we studied, a top-notch marketing manager with a superior performance record was hired into a company as a vice president "to straighten out the marketing and sales problems." The company, which was having financial difficulties, had recently been acquired by a larger corporation. The president was eager to turn it around and gave the new marketing vice president free rein—at least initially. Based on his previous experience, the new vice president correctly diagnosed that greater market share was needed for the company and that strong product management was required to bring that about. Following that logic, he made a number of pricing decisions aimed at increasing high-volume business.

When margins declined and the financial situation did not improve, however, the president increased pressure on the new vice president. Believing that the situation would eventually correct itself as the company gained back market share, the vice president resisted the pressure.

When by the second quarter, margins and profits had still failed to improve, the president took direct control over all pricing decisions and put all items on a set level of margin, regardless of volume. The new vice president began to find himself shut out by the president, and their relationship deteriorated. In fact, the vice president found the president's behavior bizarre. Unfortunately, the president's new pricing scheme also failed to increase margins, and by the fourth quarter, both the president and the vice president were fired.

What the new vice president had not known until it was too late was that improving marketing and sales had been only *one* of the president's goals. His most immediate goal had been to make the company more profitable—quickly.

Nor had the new vice president known that his boss was invested in this short-term priority for personal as well as business reasons. The president had been a strong advocate of the acquisition within the parent company, and his personal credibility was at stake.

The vice president made three basic errors. He took information supplied to him at face value, he made assumptions in areas where he had no information, and—what was most damaging—he never actively tried to clarify what his boss's objectives were. As a result, he ended up taking actions that were actually at odds with the president's priorities and objectives.

Managers who work effectively with their bosses do not behave this way. They seek out information about the boss's goals and problems and pressures. They are alert for opportunities to question the boss and others around him or her to test their assumptions. They pay attention to clues in the boss's behavior. Although it is imperative that they do this especially when they begin working with a new boss, effective managers also do this on an ongoing basis because they recognize that priorities and concerns change.

Being sensitive to a boss's work style can be crucial, especially when the boss is new. For example, a new president who was organized and formal in his approach replaced a man who was informal and intuitive. The new president worked best when he had written reports. He also preferred formal meetings with set agendas.

One of his division managers realized this need and worked with the new president to identify the kinds and frequency of information and reports that the president wanted. This manager also made a point of sending background information and brief agendas ahead of time for their discussions. He found that with this type of preparation their meetings were very useful. Another interesting result was, he found that with adequate preparation his new boss was even more effective at brainstorming problems than his more informal and intuitive predecessor had been.

In contrast, another division manager never fully understood how the new boss's work style differed from that of his predecessor. To the degree that he did sense it, he experienced it as too much control. As a result, he seldom sent the new president the background information he needed, and the president never felt fully prepared for meetings with the manager. In fact, the president spent much of the time when they met trying to get information that he felt he should have had earlier. The boss experienced these meetings as frustrating and inefficient, and the subordinate often found himself thrown off guard by the questions that the president asked. Ultimately, this division manager resigned.

The difference between the two division managers just described was not so much one of ability or even adaptability. Rather, one of the men was more sensitive to his boss's work style and to the implications of his boss's needs than the other was.

Understanding Yourself

The boss is only one-half of the relationship. You are the other half, as well as the part over which you have more direct control. Developing an effective working relationship requires, then, that you know your own needs, strengths and weaknesses, and personal style.

You are not going to change either your basic personality structure or that of your boss. But you can become aware of what it is about you that impedes or facilitates working with your boss and, with that awareness, take actions that make the relationship more effective.

For example, in one case we observed, a manager and his superior ran into problems whenever they disagreed. The boss's typical response was to harden his position and overstate it. The manager's reaction was then to raise the ante and intensify the forcefulness of his argument. In doing this, he channeled his anger into sharpening his attacks on the logical fallacies he saw in his boss's assumptions. His boss in turn would become even more adamant about holding his original position. Predictably, this escalating cycle resulted in the subordinate avoiding whenever possible any topic of potential conflict with his boss.

In discussing this problem with his peers, the manager discovered that his reaction to the boss was typical of how he generally reacted to counterarguments—but with a difference. His response would overwhelm his peers but not his boss. Because his attempts to discuss this problem with his boss were unsuccessful, he concluded that the only way to change the situation was to deal with his own instinctive reactions. Whenever the two reached an impasse, he would check his own impatience and suggest that they break up and think about it before getting together again. Usually when they renewed their discussion, they had digested their differences and were more able to work them through.

Gaining this level of self-awareness and acting on it are difficult but not impossible. For example, by reflecting over his past experiences, a young manager learned that he was not very good at dealing with difficult and emotional issues where people were involved. Because he disliked those issues and realized that his instinctive responses to them were seldom very good, he developed a habit of touching base with his boss whenever such a problem arose. Their discussions always surfaced ideas and approaches the manager had not considered. In many cases, they also identified specific actions the boss could take to help.

Although a superior–subordinate relationship is one of mutual dependence, it is also one in which the subordinate is typically more dependent on the boss than the other way around. This dependence inevitably results in the subordinate feeling a certain degree of frustration, sometimes anger, when his actions or options are constrained by his boss's decisions. This is a normal part of life and occurs in the best of relationships. The way in which a manager handles these frustrations largely depends on his or her predisposition toward dependence on authority figures.

Some people's instinctive reaction under these circumstances is to resent the boss's authority and to rebel against the boss's decisions. Sometimes a person will escalate a conflict beyond what is appropriate. Seeing the boss almost as an institutional enemy, this type of manager will often, without being conscious of it, fight with the boss just for the sake of fighting. The subordinate's reactions to being constrained are usually strong and sometimes impulsive. He or she sees the boss as someone who, by virtue of the role, is a hindrance to progress, an obstacle to be circumvented or at best tolerated.

Psychologists call this pattern of reactions counterdependent behavior. Although a counterdependent person is difficult for most superiors to manage and usually has a history of strained relationships with superiors, this sort of manager is apt to have even more trouble with a boss who tends to be directive or authoritarian. When the manager acts on his or her negative feelings, often in subtle and nonverbal ways, the boss sometimes does become the enemy. Sensing the subordinate's latent hostility, the boss will lose trust in the subordinate or his or her judgment and then behave even less openly.

Paradoxically, a manager with this type of predisposition is often a good manager of his or her own people.

He or she will many times go out of the way to get support for them and will not hesitate to go to bat for them.

At the other extreme are managers who swallow their anger and behave in a very compliant fashion when the boss makes what they know to be a poor decision. These managers will agree with the boss even when a disagreement might be welcome or when the boss would easily alter a decision if given more information. Because they bear no relationship to the specific situation at hand, their responses are as much an overreaction as those of counterdependent managers. Instead of seeing the boss as an enemy, these people deny their anger—the other extreme—and tend to see the boss as if he or she were an all-wise parent who should know best, should take responsibility for their careers, train them in all they need to know, and protect them from overly ambitious peers.

Both counterdependence and overdependence lead managers to hold unrealistic views of what a boss is. Both views ignore that bosses, like everyone else, are imperfect and fallible. They don't have unlimited time, encyclopedic knowledge, or extrasensory perception; nor are they evil enemies. They have their own pressures and concerns that are sometimes at odds with the wishes of the subordinate—and often for good reason.

Altering predispositions toward authority, especially at the extremes, is almost impossible without intensive psychotherapy (psychoanalytic theory and research suggest that such predispositions are deeply rooted in a person's personality and upbringing). However, an awareness of these extremes and the range between them can be very useful in understanding where your own predispositions fall and what the implications are for how you tend to behave in relation to your boss.

If you believe, on the one hand, that you have some tendencies toward counterdependence, you can understand and even predict what your reactions and overreactions are likely to be. If, on the other hand, you believe you have some tendencies toward overdependence, you might question the extent to which your overcompliance or inability to confront real differences may be making both you and your boss less effective.

Developing and Managing the Relationship

With a clear understanding of both your boss and yourself, you can *usually* establish a way of working together that fits both of you, that is characterized by unambiguous mutual expectations, and that helps you both be more productive and effective. The "Checklist for Managing Your Boss" summarizes some things such a relationship consists of. Following are a few more.

Checklist for Managing Your Boss

Make sure you understand your boss and his or her context, including:
- Goals and objectives
- Pressures
- Strengths, weaknesses, blind spots
- Preferred work style

Assess yourself and your needs, including:
- Strengths and weaknesses
- Personal style
- Predisposition toward dependence on authority figures

Develop and maintain a relationship that:
- Fits both your needs and styles
- Is characterized by mutual expectations
- Keeps your boss informed
- Is based on dependability and honesty
- Selectively uses your boss's time and resources

COMPATIBLE WORK STYLES

Above all else, a good working relationship with a boss
accommodates differences in work style. For example, in
one situation we studied, a manager (who had a relatively
good relationship with his superior) realized that during
meetings his boss would often become inattentive and
sometimes brusque. The subordinate's own style tended
to be discursive and exploratory. He would often digress
from the topic at hand to deal with background factors,
alternative approaches, and so forth. His boss preferred to
discuss problems with a minimum of background detail
and became impatient and distracted whenever his subordinate digressed from the immediate issue.

Recognizing this difference in style, the manager
became terser and more direct during meetings with his
boss. To help himself do this, before meetings, he would
develop brief agendas that he used as a guide. Whenever
he felt that a digression was needed, he explained why.
This small shift in his own style made these meetings
more effective and far less frustrating for both of them.

Subordinates can adjust their styles in response to
their bosses' preferred method for receiving information.
Peter Drucker divides bosses into "listeners" and "read-
ers." Some bosses like to get information in report form
so they can read and study it. Others work better with
information and reports presented in person so they can
ask questions. As Drucker points out, the implications
are obvious. If your boss is a listener, you brief him or her
in person, *then* follow it up with a memo. If your boss is a
reader, you cover important items or proposals in a
memo or report, *then* discuss them.

Other adjustments can be made according to a boss's
decision-making style. Some bosses prefer to be involved

in decisions and problems as they arise. These are high-involvement managers who like to keep their hands on the pulse of the operation. Usually their needs (and your own) are best satisfied if you touch base with them on an ad hoc basis. A boss who has a need to be involved will become involved one way or another, so there are advantages to including him or her at your initiative. Other bosses prefer to delegate—they don't want to be involved. They expect you to come to them with major problems and inform them about any important changes.

Creating a compatible relationship also involves drawing on each other's strengths and making up for each other's weaknesses. Because he knew that the boss—the vice president of engineering—was not very good at monitoring his employees' problems, one manager we studied made a point of doing it himself. The stakes were high: The engineers and technicians were all union members, the company worked on a customer-contract basis, and the company had recently experienced a serious strike.

The manager worked closely with his boss, along with people in the scheduling department and the personnel office, to make sure that potential problems were avoided. He also developed an informal arrangement through which his boss would review with him any proposed changes in personnel or assignment policies before taking action. The boss valued his advice and credited his subordinate for improving both the performance of the division and the labor–management climate.

MUTUAL EXPECTATIONS

The subordinate who passively assumes that he or she knows what the boss expects is in for trouble. Of course, some superiors will spell out their expectations very explicitly and in great detail. But most do not. And although many corporations have systems that provide a basis for communicating expectations (such as formal planning processes, career planning reviews, and performance appraisal reviews), these systems never work perfectly. Also, between these formal reviews, expectations invariably change.

Ultimately, the burden falls on the subordinate to find out what the boss's expectations are. They can be both broad (such as what kinds of problems the boss wishes to be informed about and when) as well as very specific (such things as when a particular project should be completed and what kinds of information the boss needs in the interim).

Getting a boss who tends to be vague or not explicit to express expectations can be difficult. But effective managers find ways to get that information. Some will draft a detailed memo covering key aspects of their work and then send it to their boss for approval. They then follow this up with a face-to-face discussion in which they go over each item in the memo. A discussion like this will often surface virtually all of the boss's expectations.

Other effective managers will deal with an inexplicit boss by initiating an ongoing series of informal discussions about "good management" and "our objectives." Still others find useful information more indirectly through those who used to work for the boss and through the formal planning systems in which the boss makes commitments to his or her own superior. Which approach you choose, of course, should depend on your understanding of your boss's style.

Developing a workable set of mutual expectations also requires that you communicate your own expectations to the boss, find out if they are realistic, and influence the boss to accept the ones that are important to you. Being able to influence the boss to value your expectations can be particularly important if the boss is an overachiever. Such a boss will often set unrealistically high standards that need to be brought into line with reality.

A FLOW OF INFORMATION

How much information a boss needs about what a subordinate is doing will vary significantly depending on the boss's style, the situation he or she is in, and the confidence the boss has in the subordinate. But it is not uncommon for a boss to need more information than the subordinate would naturally supply or for the subordinate to think the boss knows more than he or she really does. Effective managers recognize that they probably underestimate what their bosses need to know and make sure they find ways to keep them informed through processes that fit their styles.

Managing the flow of information upward is particularly difficult if the boss does not like to hear about problems. Although many people would deny it, bosses often give off signals that they want to hear only good news. They show great displeasure—usually nonverbally—when someone tells them about a problem. Ignoring individual achievement, they may even evaluate more favorably subordinates who do not bring problems to them.

Nevertheless, for the good of the organization, the boss, and the subordinate, a superior needs to hear about failures as well as successes. Some subordinates deal with a good-news-only boss by finding indirect ways to get the necessary information to him or her, such as a management information system. Others see to it that potential problems, whether in the form of good surprises or bad news, are communicated immediately.

DEPENDABILITY AND HONESTY

Few things are more disabling to a boss than a subordinate on whom he cannot depend, whose work he cannot trust. Almost no one is intentionally undependable, but many managers are inadvertently so because of oversight or uncertainty about the boss's priorities. A commitment to an optimistic delivery date may please a superior in the short term but become a source of displeasure if not honored. It's difficult for a boss to rely on a subordinate who repeatedly slips deadlines. As one president (describing a subordinate) put it: "I'd rather he be more consistent even if he delivered fewer peak successes—at least I could rely on him."

Nor are many managers intentionally dishonest with their bosses. But it is easy to shade the truth and play down issues. Current concerns often become future surprise problems. It's almost impossible for bosses to work effectively if they cannot rely on a fairly accurate reading from their subordinates. Because it undermines credibility, dishonesty is perhaps the most troubling trait a subordinate can have. Without a basic level of trust, a boss feels compelled to check all of a subordinate's decisions, which makes it difficult to delegate.

GOOD USE OF TIME AND RESOURCES

Your boss is probably as limited in his or her store of time, energy, and influence as you are. Every request you make of your boss uses up some of these resources, so it's wise to draw on these resources selectively. This may sound obvious, but many managers use up their boss's time (and some of their own credibility) over relatively trivial issues.

One vice president went to great lengths to get his boss to fire a meddlesome secretary in another department. His boss had to use considerable influence to do it. Understandably, the head of the other department was not pleased. Later, when the vice president wanted to tackle more important problems, he ran into trouble. By using up blue chips on a relatively trivial issue, he had made it difficult for him and his boss to meet more important goals.

No doubt, some subordinates will resent that on top of all their other duties, they also need to take time and energy to manage their relationships with their bosses. Such managers fail to realize the importance of this activity and how it can simplify their jobs by eliminating potentially severe problems. Effective managers recognize that this part of their work is legitimate. Seeing themselves as ultimately responsible for what they achieve in an organization, they know they need to establish and manage relationships with everyone on whom they depend—and that includes the boss.

Originally published January–February 1980
Reprint R0501J

The Core Competence of the Corporation

C.K. PRAHALAD AND GARY HAMEL

Executive Summary

IN THE EARLY 1980s, GTE was positioned to become a major player in the information technology industry. NEC was much smaller and had no experience as an operating telecommunications company. Today NEC is among the top five companies in telecommunications, semiconductors, and mainframes. GTE has become essentially a telephone company with a position in defense and lighting products.

What happened? NEC built and nurtured a group of core competencies. GTE, on the other hand, couldn't agree on which competencies to base its strategy. It organized itself around strategic business units, which by nature underinvest in core competencies, imprison resources, and bind innovation.

133

A company's competitiveness derives from its core competencies and core products (the tangible results of core competencies). Core competence is the collective learning in the organization, especially the capacity to coordinate diverse production skills and integrate streams of technologies. It is also a commitment to working across organizational boundaries.

Organizing around core competencies requires a radical change in corporate organization. The first step requires identifying core competencies, which meet these three requirements: they provide potential access to a wide variety of markets, make a contribution to the customer benefits of the product, and are difficult for competitors to imitate.

The next step is to redesign the architecture of the company and provide an impetus for learning from alliances and a focus for internal development. Management should ask: How long could we preserve our competitiveness if we did not control this core competence? How central is this core competence to customer benefits? What opportunities would be foreclosed if we lost this competence?

THE MOST POWERFUL WAY to prevail in global competition is still invisible to many companies. During the 1980s, top executives were judged on their ability to restructure, declutter, and delayer their corporations. In the 1990s, they'll be judged on their ability to identify, cultivate, and exploit the core competencies that make growth possible—indeed, they'll have to rethink the concept of the corporation itself.

Consider the last ten years of GTE and NEC. In the early 1980s, GTE was well positioned to become a major player in the evolving information technology industry. It was active in telecommunications. Its operations spanned a variety of businesses including telephones, switching and transmission systems, digital PABX, semiconductors, packet switching, satellites, defense systems, and lighting products. And GTE's Entertainment Products Group, which produced Sylvania color TVs, had a position in related display technologies. In 1980, GTE's sales were $9.98 billion, and net cash flow was $1.73 billion. NEC, in contrast, was much smaller, at $3.8 billion in sales. It had a comparable technological base and computer businesses, but it had no experience as an operating telecommunications company.

Yet look at the positions of GTE and NEC in 1988. GTE's 1988 sales were $16.46 billion, and NEC's sales were considerably higher at $21.89 billion. GTE has, in effect, become a telephone operating company with a position in defense and lighting products. GTE's other businesses are small in global terms. GTE has divested Sylvania TV and Telenet, put switching, transmission, and digital PABX into joint ventures, and closed down semiconductors. As a result, the international position of GTE has eroded. Non-U.S. revenue as a percent of total revenue dropped from 20% to 15% between 1980 and 1988.

NEC has emerged as the world leader in semiconductors and as a first-tier player in telecommunications products and computers. It has consolidated its position in mainframe computers. It has moved beyond public switching and transmission to include such lifestyle products as mobile telephones, facsimile machines, and laptop computers—bridging the gap between telecommunications and office automation. NEC is the only company in the world to be in the top five in revenue in telecommunications, semiconductors, and mainframes. Why did these two companies, starting with comparable business portfolios, perform so differently? Largely because NEC conceived of itself in terms of "core competencies," and GTE did not.

Rethinking the Corporation

Once, the diversified corporation could simply point its business units at particular end product markets and admonish them to become world leaders. But with market boundaries changing ever more quickly, targets are elusive and capture is at best temporary. A few companies have proven themselves adept at inventing new markets, quickly entering emerging markets, and dramatically shifting patterns of customer choice in established markets. These are the ones to emulate. The critical task for management is to create an organization capable of infusing products with irresistible functionality or, better yet, creating products that customers need but have not yet even imagined.

This is a deceptively difficult task. Ultimately, it requires radical change in the management of major companies. It means, first of all, that top managements of Western companies must assume responsibility for competitive decline. Everyone knows about high interest rates, Japanese protectionism, outdated antitrust laws, obstreperous unions, and impatient investors. What is harder to see, or harder to acknowledge, is how little added momentum companies actually get from political or macroeconomic "relief." Both the theory and practice of Western management have created a drag on our forward motion. It is the principles of management that are in need of reform.

NEC versus GTE, again, is instructive and only one of many such comparative cases we analyzed to understand the changing basis for global leadership. Early in the 1970s, NEC articulated a strategic intent to exploit the convergence of computing and communications, what it called "C&C."[1] Success, top management reckoned, would hinge on acquiring *competencies*, particularly in semiconductors. Management adopted an appropriate "strategic architecture," summarized by C&C, and then communicated its intent to the whole organization and the outside world during the mid-1970s.

NEC constituted a "C&C Committee" of top managers to oversee the development of core products and core competencies. NEC put in place coordination groups and committees that cut across the interests of individual businesses. Consistent with its strategic architecture, NEC shifted enormous resources to strengthen its position in components and central processors. By using collaborative arrangements to multiply internal resources, NEC was able to accumulate a broad array of core competencies.

NEC carefully identified three interrelated streams of technological and market evolution. Top management determined that computing would evolve from large mainframes to distributed processing, components from simple ICs to VLSI, and communications from mechanical cross-bar exchange to complex digital systems we now call ISDN. As things evolved further, NEC reasoned, the computing, communications, and components businesses would so overlap that it would be very hard to distinguish among them, and that there would be enormous opportunities for any company that had built the competencies needed to serve all three markets.

NEC top management determined that semiconductors would be the company's most important "core product." It entered into myriad strategic alliances—over 100 as of 1987—aimed at building competencies rapidly and at low cost. In mainframe computers, its most noted relationship was with Honeywell and Bull. Almost all the collaborative arrangements in the semiconductor-component field were oriented toward technology access. As they entered collaborative arrangements, NEC's operating managers understood the rationale for these alliances and the goal of internalizing partner skills. NEC's director of research summed up its competence acquisition during the 1970s and 1980s this way: "From an investment standpoint, it was much quicker and cheaper to use foreign technology. There wasn't a need for us to develop new ideas."

No such clarity of strategic intent and strategic architecture appeared to exist at GTE. Although senior executives discussed the implications of the evolving information technology industry, no commonly accepted view of which competencies would be required to compete in that industry were communicated widely. While significant staff work was done to identify key technologies, senior line managers continued to act as if they were managing independent business units. Decentralization made it difficult to focus on core competencies. Instead, individual businesses became increasingly dependent on outsiders for critical skills, and collaboration became a route to staged exits. Today, with a new management team in place, GTE has repositioned itself to apply its competencies to emerging markets in telecommunications services.

The Roots of Competitive Advantage

The distinction we observed in the way NEC and GTE conceived of themselves—a portfolio of competencies versus a portfolio of businesses—was repeated across many industries. From 1980 to 1988, Canon grew by 264%, Honda by 200%. Compare that with Xerox and Chrysler. And if Western managers were once anxious about the low cost and high quality of Japanese imports, they are now overwhelmed by the pace at which Japanese rivals are inventing new markets, creating new products, and enhancing them. Canon has given us personal copiers; Honda has moved from motorcycles to four-wheel off-road buggies. Sony developed the 8mm camcorder, Yamaha, the digital piano. Komatsu developed an underwater remote-controlled bulldozer, while Casio's latest gambit is a small-screen color LCD television. Who would have anticipated the evolution of these vanguard markets?

In more established markets, the Japanese challenge has been just as disquieting. Japanese companies are generating a blizzard of features and functional enhancements that bring technological sophistication to everyday products. Japanese car producers have been pioneering four-wheel steering, four-valve-per-cylinder engines, in-car navigation systems, and sophisticated electronic engine-management systems. On the strength of its product features, Canon is now a player in facsimile transmission machines, desktop laser printers, even semiconductor manufacturing equipment.

In the short run, a company's competitiveness derives from the price/performance attributes of current products. But the survivors of the first wave of global competition, Western and Japanese alike, are all converging on similar and formidable standards for product cost and quality—minimum hurdles for continued competition, but less and less important as sources of differential advantage. In the long run, competitiveness derives from an ability to build, at lower cost and more speedily than competitors, the core competencies that spawn unanticipated products. The real sources of advantage are to be found in management's ability to consolidate corporatewide technologies and production skills into competencies that empower individual businesses to adapt quickly to changing opportunities.

Senior executives who claim that they cannot build core competencies either because they feel the autonomy of business units is sacrosanct or because their feet are held to the quarterly budget fire should think again. The problem in many Western companies is not that their senior executives are any less capable than those in Japan nor that Japanese companies possess greater technical capabilities. Instead, it is their adherence to a concept of the corporation that unnecessarily limits the ability of individual businesses to fully exploit the deep reservoir of technological capability that many American and European companies possess.

The diversified corporation is a large tree. The trunk and major limbs are core products, the smaller branches are business units; the leaves, flowers, and fruit are end products. The root system that provides nourishment, sustenance, and stability is the core competence. You can miss the strength of competitors by looking only at their end products, in the same way you miss the strength of a tree if you look only at its leaves. (See the chart "Competencies: The Roots of Competitiveness.")

Core competencies are the collective learning in the organization, especially how to coordinate diverse production skills and integrate multiple streams of technologies. Consider Sony's capacity to miniaturize or Philips's optical-media expertise. The theoretical knowledge to put a radio on a chip does not in itself assure a company the skill to produce a miniature radio no bigger than a business card. To bring off this feat, Casio must harmonize know-how in miniaturization, microprocessor design, material science, and ultrathin precision

Competencies: The Roots of Competitiveness

The corporation, like a tree, grows from its roots. Core products are nourished by competencies and engender business units, whose fruit are end products.

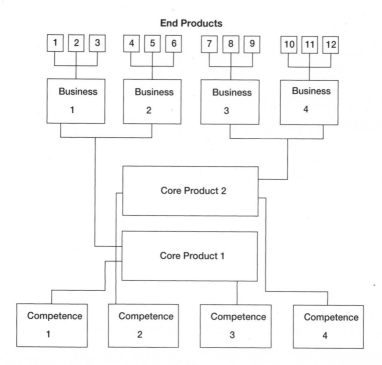

casing—the same skills it applies in its miniature card calculators, pocket TVs, and digital watches.

If core competence is about harmonizing streams of technology, it is also about the organization of work and the delivery of value. Among Sony's competencies is miniaturization. To bring miniaturization to its products, Sony must ensure that technologists, engineers, and marketers have a shared understanding of customer needs and of technological possibilities. The force of core competence is felt as decisively in services as in manufacturing. Citicorp was ahead of others investing in an operating system that allowed it to participate in world markets 24 hours a day. Its competence in systems has provided the company the means to differentiate itself from many financial service institutions.

Core competence is communication, involvement, and a deep commitment to working across organizational boundaries. It involves many levels of people and all functions. World-class research in, for example, lasers or ceramics can take place in corporate laboratories without having an impact on any of the businesses of the company. The skills that together constitute core competence must coalesce around individuals whose efforts are not so narrowly focused that they cannot recognize the opportunities for blending their functional expertise with those of others in new and interesting ways.

Core competence does not diminish with use. Unlike physical assets, which do deteriorate over time, competencies are enhanced as they are applied and shared. But competencies still need to be nurtured and protected; knowledge fades if it is not used. Competencies are the glue that binds existing businesses. They are also the engine for new business development. Patterns of diversification and market entry may be guided by them, not just by the attractiveness of markets.

Consider 3M's competence with sticky tape. In dreaming up businesses as diverse as "Post-it" notes, magnetic tape, photographic film, pressure-sensitive tapes, and coated abrasives, the company has brought to bear widely shared competencies in substrates, coatings, and adhesives and devised various ways to combine them. Indeed, 3M has invested consistently in them. What seems to be an extremely diversified portfolio of businesses belies a few shared core competencies.

In contrast, there are major companies that have had the potential to build core competencies but failed to do so because top management was unable to conceive of the company as anything other than a collection of discrete businesses. GE sold much of its consumer electronics business to Thomson of France, arguing that it was becoming increasingly difficult to maintain its competitiveness in this sector. That was undoubtedly so, but it is ironic that it sold several key businesses to competitors who were already competence leaders—Black & Decker in small electrical motors, and Thomson, which was eager to build its competence in microelectronics and had learned from the Japanese that a position in consumer electronics was vital to this challenge.

Management trapped in the strategic business unit (SBU) mind-set almost inevitably finds its individual businesses dependent on external sources for critical components, such as motors or compressors. But these are not just components. They are core products that contribute to the competitiveness of a wide range of end products. They are the physical embodiments of core competencies.

How Not to Think of Competence

Since companies are in a race to build the competencies that determine global leadership, successful companies have stopped imagining themselves as bundles of businesses making products. Canon, Honda, Casio, or NEC may seem to preside over portfolios of businesses unrelated in terms of customers, distribution channels, and merchandising strategy. Indeed, they have portfolios that may seem idiosyncratic at times: NEC is the only global company to be among leaders in computing, telecommunications, and semiconductors *and* to have a thriving consumer electronics business.

But looks are deceiving. In NEC, digital technology, especially VLSI and systems integration skills, is fundamental. In the core competencies underlying them, disparate businesses become coherent. It is Honda's core competence in engines and power trains that gives it a distinctive advantage in car, motorcycle, lawn mower, and generator businesses. Canon's core competencies in optics, imaging, and microprocessor controls have enabled it to enter, even dominate, markets as seemingly diverse as copiers, laser printers, cameras, and image scanners. Philips worked for more than 15 years to perfect its optical-media (laser disc) competence, as did JVC in building a leading position in video recording. Other examples of core competencies might include mechantronics (the ability to marry mechanical and electronic engineering), video displays, bioengineering, and microelectronics. In the early stages of its competence building, Philips could not have imagined all the products that would be spawned by its optical-media competence, nor could JVC have anticipated miniature camcorders when it first began exploring videotape technologies.

Unlike the battle for global brand dominance, which is visible in the world's broadcast and print media and is aimed at building global "share of mind," the battle to build world-class competencies is invisible to people who aren't deliberately looking for it. Top management often tracks the cost and quality of competitors' products, yet how many managers untangle the web of alliances their Japanese competitors have constructed to acquire competencies at low cost? In how many Western boardrooms is there an explicit, shared understanding of the competencies the company must build for world leadership? Indeed, how many senior executives discuss the crucial distinction between competitive strategy at the level of a business and competitive strategy at the level of an entire company?

Let us be clear. Cultivating core competence does not mean outspending rivals on research and development. In 1983, when Canon surpassed Xerox in worldwide unit market share in the copier business, its R&D budget in reprographics was but a small fraction of Xerox's. Over the past 20 years, NEC has spent less on R&D as a percentage of sales than almost all of its American and European competitors.

Nor does core competence mean shared costs, as when two or more SBUs use a common facility—a plant, service facility, or sales force—or share a common component. The gains of sharing may be substantial, but the search for shared costs is typically a post hoc effort to rationalize production across existing businesses, not a premeditated effort to build the competencies out of which the businesses themselves grow.

Building core competencies is more ambitious and different than integrating vertically, moreover. Managers deciding whether to make or buy will start with end products and look upstream to the efficiencies of the supply chain and downstream toward distribution and customers. They do not take inventory of skills and look forward to applying them in nontraditional ways. (Of course, decisions about competencies *do* provide a logic for vertical integration. Canon is not particularly integrated in its copier business, except in those aspects of the vertical chain that support the competencies it regards as critical.)

Identifying Core Competencies—and Losing Them

At least three tests can be applied to identify core competencies in a company. First, a core competence provides potential access to a wide variety of markets. Competence in display systems, for example, enables a company to participate in such diverse businesses as calculators, miniature TV sets, monitors for laptop computers, and automotive dashboards—which is why Casio's entry into the handheld TV market was predictable. Second, a core competence should make a significant contribution to the perceived customer benefits of the end product. Clearly, Honda's engine expertise fills this bill.

Finally, a core competence should be difficult for competitors to imitate. And it *will* be difficult if it is a complex harmonization of individual technologies and production skills. A rival might acquire some of the technologies that comprise the core competence, but it will find it more difficult to duplicate the more or less comprehensive pattern of internal coordination and learning. JVC's decision in the early 1960s to pursue the development of a videotape competence passed the three tests outlined here. RCA's decision in the late 1970s to develop a stylus-based video turntable system did not.

Few companies are likely to build world leadership in more than five or six fundamental competencies. A company that compiles a list of 20 to 30 capabilities has probably not produced a list of core competencies. Still, it is probably a good discipline to generate a list of this sort and to see aggregate capabilities as building blocks. This tends to prompt the search for licensing deals and alliances through which the company may acquire, at low cost, missing pieces.

Most Western companies hardly think about competitiveness in these terms at all. It is time to take a tough-minded look at the risks they are running. Companies that judge competitiveness, their own and their competitors', primarily in terms of the price/performance of end products are courting the erosion of core competencies— or making too little effort to enhance them. The embedded skills that give rise to the next generation of competitive products cannot be "rented in" by outsourcing and OEM-supply relationships. In our view, too many companies have unwittingly surrendered core competencies when they cut internal investment in what they mistakenly thought were just "cost centers" in favor of outside suppliers.

Consider Chrysler. Unlike Honda, it has tended to view engines and power trains as simply one more component. Chrysler is becoming increasingly dependent on Mitsubishi and Hyundai: between 1985 and 1987, the number of outsourced engines went from 252,000 to 382,000. It is difficult to imagine Honda yielding manufacturing responsibility, much less design, of so critical a part of a car's function to an outside company—which is why Honda has made such an enormous commitment to

Formula One auto racing. Honda has been able to pool its engine-related technologies; it has parlayed these into a corporatewide competency from which it develops world-beating products, despite R&D budgets smaller than those of GM and Toyota.

Of course, it is perfectly possible for a company to have a competitive product line up but be a laggard in developing core competencies—at least for a while. If a company wanted to enter the copier business today, it would find a dozen Japanese companies more than willing to supply copiers on the basis of an OEM private label. But when fundamental technologies changed or if its supplier decided to enter the market directly and become a competitor, that company's product line, along with all of its investments in marketing and distribution, could be vulnerable. Outsourcing can provide a shortcut to a more competitive product, but it typically contributes little to building the people-embodied skills that are needed to sustain product leadership.

Nor is it possible for a company to have an intelligent alliance or sourcing strategy if it has not made a choice about where it will build competence leadership. Clearly, Japanese companies have benefited from alliances. They've used them to learn from Western partners who were not fully committed to preserving core competencies of their own. As we've argued in these pages before, learning within an alliance takes a positive commitment of resources—the travel, a pool of dedicated people, test-bed facilities, time to internalize and test what has been learned.[2] A company may not make this effort if it doesn't have clear goals for competence building.

Another way of losing is forgoing opportunities to establish competencies that are evolving in existing businesses. In the 1970s and 1980s, many American and

European companies—like GE, Motorola, GTE, Thorn, and GEC—chose to exit the color television business, which they regarded as mature. If by "mature" they meant that they had run out of new product ideas at precisely the moment global rivals had targeted the TV business for entry, then yes, the industry was mature. But it certainly wasn't mature in the sense that all opportunities to enhance and apply video-based competencies had been exhausted.

In ridding themselves of their television businesses, these companies failed to distinguish between divesting the business and destroying their video media-based competencies. They not only got out of the TV business but they also closed the door on a whole stream of future opportunities reliant on video-based competencies. The television industry, considered by many U.S. companies in the 1970s to be unattractive, is today the focus of a fierce public policy debate about the inability of U.S. corporations to benefit from the $20-billion-a-year opportunity that HDTV will represent in the mid- to late 1990s. Ironically, the U.S. government is being asked to fund a massive research project—in effect, to compensate U.S. companies for their failure to preserve critical core competencies when they had the chance.

In contrast, one can see a company like Sony reducing its emphasis on VCRs (where it has not been very successful and where Korean companies now threaten), without reducing its commitment to video-related competencies. Sony's Betamax led to a debacle. But it emerged with its videotape recording competencies intact and is currently challenging Matsushita in the 8mm camcorder market.

There are two clear lessons here. First, the costs of losing a core competence can be only partly calculated in advance. The baby may be thrown out with the bath water in divestment decisions. Second, since core competencies are built through a process of continuous improvement and enhancement that may span a decade or longer, a company that has failed to invest in core competence building will find it very difficult to enter an emerging market, unless, of course, it will be content simply to serve as a distribution channel.

American semiconductor companies like Motorola learned this painful lesson when they elected to forgo direct participation in the 256k generation of DRAM chips. Having skipped this round, Motorola, like most of its American competitors, needed a large infusion of technical help from Japanese partners to rejoin the battle in the 1-megabyte generation. When it comes to core competencies, it is difficult to get off the train, walk to the next station, and then reboard.

From Core Competencies to Core Products

The tangible link between identified core competencies and end products is what we call the core products—the physical embodiments of one or more core competencies. Honda's engines, for example, are core products, linchpins between design and development skills that ultimately lead to a proliferation of end products. Core products are the components or subassemblies that actually contribute to the value of the end products. Thinking in terms of core products forces a company to distinguish between the brand share it achieves in end product markets (for example, 40% of the U.S. refrigerator market) and the manufacturing share it achieves in any particular core product (for example, 5% of the world share of compressor output).

Canon is reputed to have an 84% world manufacturing share in desktop laser printer "engines," even though its brand share in the laser printer business is minuscule. Similarly, Matsushita has a world manufacturing share of about 45% in key VCR components, far in excess of its brand share (Panasonic, JVC, and others) of 20%. And Matsushita has a commanding core product share in compressors worldwide, estimated at 40%, even though its brand share in both the air-conditioning and refrigerator businesses is quite small.

It is essential to make this distinction between core competencies, core products, and end products because global competition is played out by different rules and for different stakes at each level. To build or defend leadership over the long term, a corporation will probably be a winner at each level. At the level of core competence, the goal is to build world leadership in the design and development of a particular class of product functionality— be it compact data storage and retrieval, as with Philips's optical-media competence, or compactness and ease of use, as with Sony's micromotors and microprocessor controls.

To sustain leadership in their chosen core competence areas, these companies *seek to maximize their world manufacturing share in core products.* The manufacture of core products for a wide variety of external (and internal) customers yields the revenue and market feedback that, at least partly, determines the pace at which core competencies can be enhanced and extended. This thinking was behind JVC's decision in the mid-1970s to establish VCR supply relationships with leading national consumer electronics companies in Europe and the United States. In supplying Thomson, Thorn, and Telefunken (all independent companies at

152   *Prahalad and Hamel*

that time) as well as U.S. partners, JVC was able to gain
the cash and the diversity of market experience that ultimately enabled it to outpace Philips and Sony. (Philips
developed videotape competencies in parallel with JVC,
but it failed to build a worldwide network of OEM relationships that would have allowed it to accelerate the
refinement of its videotape competence through the sale
of core products.)

JVC's success has not been lost on Korean companies
like Goldstar, Samsung, Kia, and Daewoo, who are building core product leadership in areas as diverse as displays, semiconductors, and automotive engines through
their OEM-supply contracts with Western companies.
Their avowed goal is to capture investment initiative
away from potential competitors, often U.S. companies.
In doing so, they accelerate their competence-building
efforts while "hollowing out" their competitors. By focusing on competence and embedding it in core products,
Asian competitors have built up advantages in component markets first and have then leveraged off their superior products to move downstream to build brand share.
And they are not likely to remain the low-cost suppliers
forever. As their reputation for brand leadership is consolidated, they may well gain price leadership. Honda has
proven this with its Acura line, and other Japanese car
makers are following suit.

Control over core products is critical for other reasons. A dominant position in core products allows a
company to shape the evolution of applications and end
markets. Such compact audio disc–related core products
as data drives and lasers have enabled Sony and Philips
to influence the evolution of the computer-peripheral
business in optical-media storage. As a company mul-
tiplies the number of application arenas for its core

products, it can consistently reduce the cost, time, and risk in new product development. In short, well-targeted core products can lead to economies of scale *and* scope.

The Tyranny of the SBU

The new terms of competitive engagement cannot be understood using analytical tools devised to manage the diversified corporation of 20 years ago, when competition was primarily domestic (GE versus Westinghouse, General Motors versus Ford) and all the key players were speaking the language of the same business schools and consultancies. Old prescriptions have potentially toxic side effects. The need for new principles is most obvious

---

Two Concepts of the Corporation: SBU or Core Competence

	SBU	**Core Competence**
Basis for competition	Competitiveness of today's products	Interfirm competition to build competencies
Corporate structure	Portfolio of businesses related in product-market terms	Portfolio of competencies, core products, and businesses
Status of the business unit	Autonomy is sacrosanct; the SBU "owns" all resources other than cash	SBU is a potential reservoir of core competencies
Resource allocation	Discrete businesses are the unit of analysis; capital is allocated business by business	Businesses and competencies are the unit of analysis: top management allocates capital and talent
Value added of top management	Optimizing corporate returns through capital allocation trade-offs among businesses	Enunciating strategic architecture and building competencies to secure the future

in companies organized exclusively according to the logic of SBUs. The implications of the two alternate concepts of the corporation are summarized in "Two Concepts of the Corporation: SBU or Core Competence."

Obviously, diversified corporations have a portfolio of products and a portfolio of businesses. But we believe in a view of the company as a portfolio of competencies as well. U.S. companies do not lack the technical resources to build competencies, but their top management often lacks the vision to build them and the administrative means for assembling resources spread across multiple businesses. A shift in commitment will inevitably influence patterns of diversification, skill deployment, resource allocation priorities, and approaches to alliances and outsourcing.

We have described the three different planes on which battles for global leadership are waged: core competence, core products, and end products. A corporation has to know whether it is winning or losing on each plane. By sheer weight of investment, a company might be able to beat its rivals to blue-sky technologies yet still lose the race to build core competence leadership. If a company is winning the race to build core competencies (as opposed to building leadership in a few technologies), it will almost certainly outpace rivals in new business development. If a company is winning the race to capture world manufacturing share in core products, it will probably outpace rivals in improving product features and the price/performance ratio.

Determining whether one is winning or losing end product battles is more difficult because measures of product market share do not necessarily reflect various companies' underlying competitiveness. Indeed, companies that attempt to build market share by relying on the competitiveness of others, rather than investing in core competencies and world core-product leadership, may be treading on quicksand. In the race for global brand dominance, companies like 3M, Black & Decker, Canon, Honda, NEC, and Citicorp have built global brand umbrellas by proliferating products out of their core competencies. This has allowed their individual businesses to build image, customer loyalty, and access to distribution channels.

When you think about this reconceptualization of the corporation, the primacy of the SBU—an organizational dogma for a generation—is now clearly an anachronism. Where the SBU is an article of faith, resistance to the seductions of decentralization can seem heretical. In many companies, the SBU prism means that only one plane of the global competitive battle, the battle to put competitive products on the shelf *today,* is visible to top management. What are the costs of this distortion?

Underinvestment in Developing Core Competencies and Core Products. When the organization is conceived of as a multiplicity of SBUs, no single business may feel responsible for maintaining a viable position in core products nor be able to justify the investment required to build world leadership in some core competence. In the absence of a more comprehensive view imposed by corporate management, SBU managers will tend to underinvest. Recently, companies such as Kodak and Philips have recognized this as a potential problem and have begun searching for new organizational forms that will allow them to develop and manufacture core products for both internal and external customers.

SBU managers have traditionally conceived of competitors in the same way they've seen themselves. On the whole, they've failed to note the emphasis Asian competitors were placing on building leadership in core products or to understand the critical linkage between world manufacturing leadership and the ability to sustain development pace in core competence. They've failed to pursue OEM-supply opportunities or to look across their various product divisions in an attempt to identify opportunities for coordinated initiatives.

Imprisoned Resources. As an SBU evolves, it often develops unique competencies. Typically, the people who embody this competence are seen as the sole property of the business in which they grew up. The manager of another SBU who asks to borrow talented people is likely to get a cold rebuff. SBU managers are not only unwilling to lend their competence carriers but they may actually hide talent to prevent its redeployment in the pursuit of new opportunities. This may be compared to residents of an underdeveloped country hiding most of their cash under their mattresses. The benefits of competencies, like the benefits of the money supply, depend on the velocity of their circulation as well as on the size of the stock the company holds.

Western companies have traditionally had an advantage in the stock of skills they possess. But have they been able to reconfigure them quickly to respond to new opportunities? Canon, NEC, and Honda have had a lesser stock of the people and technologies that compose core competencies but could move them much quicker from one business unit to another. Corporate R&D spending at Canon is not fully indicative of the size of Canon's core competence stock and tells the casual observer nothing about the velocity with which Canon is able to move core competencies to exploit opportunities.

When competencies become imprisoned, the people who carry the competencies do not get assigned to the most exciting opportunities, and their skills begin to atrophy. Only by fully leveraging core competencies can small companies like Canon afford to compete with industry giants like Xerox. How strange that SBU managers, who are perfectly willing to compete for cash in the capital budgeting process, are unwilling to compete for people—the company's most precious asset. We find it ironic that top management devotes so much attention to the capital budgeting process yet typically has no comparable mechanism for allocating the human skills that embody core competencies. Top managers are seldom able to look four or five levels down into the organization, identify the people who embody critical competencies, and move them across organizational boundaries.

Bounded Innovation. If core competencies are not recognized, individual SBUs will pursue only those innovation opportunities that are close at hand—marginal product-line extensions or geographic expansions. Hybrid opportunities like fax machines, laptop computers, hand-held televisions, or portable music keyboards will emerge only when managers take off their SBU blinkers. Remember, Canon appeared to be in the camera business at the time it was preparing to become a world leader in copiers. Conceiving of the corporation in terms of core competencies widens the domain of innovation.

Developing Strategic Architecture

The fragmentation of core competencies becomes inevitable when a diversified company's information systems, patterns of communication, career paths, managerial rewards, and processes of strategy development do not transcend SBU lines. We believe that senior management should spend a significant amount of its time developing a corporatewide strategic architecture that establishes objectives for competence building. A strategic architecture is a road map of the future that identifies which core competencies to build and their constituent technologies.

By providing an impetus for learning from alliances and a focus for internal development efforts, a strategic architecture like NEC's C&C can dramatically reduce the investment needed to secure future market leadership. How can a company make partnerships intelligently without a clear understanding of the core competencies it is trying to build and those it is attempting to prevent from being unintentionally transferred?

Of course, all of this begs the question of what a strategic architecture should look like. The answer will be different for every company. But it is helpful to think again of that tree, of the corporation organized around core products and, ultimately, core competencies. To sink sufficiently strong roots, a company must answer some fundamental questions: How long could we preserve our competitiveness in this business if we did not control this particular core competence? How central is this core competence to perceived customer benefits? What future opportunities would be foreclosed if we were to lose this particular competence?

The architecture provides a logic for product and market diversification, moreover. An SBU manager would be asked: Does the new market opportunity add to the overall goal of becoming the best player in the world? Does it exploit or add to the core competence? At Vickers, for example, diversification options have been judged in the context of becoming the best power and motion control company in the world (see the insert "Vickers Learns the Value of Strategic Architecture" at the end of this article).

The strategic architecture should make resource allocation priorities transparent to the entire organization. It provides a template for allocation decisions by top management. It helps lower level managers understand the logic of allocation priorities and disciplines senior management to maintain consistency. In short, it yields a definition of the company and the markets it serves. 3M, Vickers, NEC, Canon, and Honda all qualify on this score. Honda *knew* it was exploiting what it had learned from motorcycles— how to make high-revving, smooth-running, lightweight engines—when it entered the car business. The task of creating a strategic architecture forces the organization to identify and commit to the technical and production linkages across SBUs that will provide a distinct competitive advantage.

It is consistency of resource allocation and the development of an administrative infrastructure appropriate to it that breathes life into a strategic architecture and creates a managerial culture, teamwork, a capacity to change, and a willingness to share resources, to protect proprietary skills, and to think long term. That is also the reason the specific architecture cannot be copied easily or overnight by competitors. Strategic architecture is a tool for communicating with customers and other external constituents. It reveals the broad direction without giving away every step.

Redeploying to Exploit Competencies

If the company's core competencies are its critical resource and if top management must ensure that competence carriers are not held hostage by some particular business, then it follows that SBUs should bid for core competencies in the same way they bid for capital. We've made this point glancingly. It is important enough to consider more deeply.

Once top management (with the help of divisional and SBU managers) has identified overarching competencies, it must ask businesses to identify the projects and people closely connected with them. Corporate officers should direct an audit of the location, number, and quality of the people who embody competence.

This sends an important signal to middle managers: core competencies are corporate resources and may be reallocated by *corporate* management. An individual business doesn't own anybody. SBUs are entitled to the services of individual employees so long as SBU management can demonstrate that the opportunity it is pursuing yields the highest possible pay-off on the investment in their skills. This message is further underlined if each year in the strategic planning or budgeting process, unit managers must justify their hold on the people who carry the company's core competencies.

Elements of Canon's core competence in optics are spread across businesses as diverse as cameras, copiers, and semiconductor lithographic equipment and are shown in "Core Competencies at Canon." When Canon identified an opportunity in digital laser printers, it gave SBU managers the right to raid other SBUs to pull together the required pool of talent. When Canon's reprographics products division undertook to develop microprocessor-controlled copiers, it turned to the photo products group, which had developed the world's first microprocessor-controlled camera.

Core Competencies at Canon

Every Canon product is the result of at least one core competency.

	Precision Mechanics	Fine Optics	Micro-electronics
Basic camera	■	☐	
Compact fashion camera	■	☐	
Electronic camera	■	☐	
EOS autofocus camera	■	☐	■
Video still camera	■	☐	■
Laser beam printer	■	☐	■
Color video printer	■		■
Bubble jet printer	■		■
Basic fax	■		■
Laser fax	■		■
Calculator			■
Plain paper copier	■	☐	■
Battery PPC	■	☐	■
Color copier	■	☐	■
Laser copier	■	☐	■
Color laser copier	■	☐	■
NAVI	■	☐	■
Still video system	■	☐	■
Laser imager	■	☐	■
Cell analyzer	■	☐	■
Mask aligners	■		■
Stepper aligners	■		■
Excimer laser aligners	■	☐	■

Also reward systems that focus only on product-line results and career paths that seldom cross SBU boundaries engender patterns of behavior among unit managers that are destructively competitive. At NEC, divisional managers come together to identify next-generation competencies. Together they decide how much investment needs to be made to build up each future competency and the contribution in capital and staff support that each division will need to make. There is also a sense of equitable exchange. One division may make a disproportionate contribution or may benefit less from the progress made, but such short-term inequalities will balance out over the long term.

Incidentally, the positive contribution of the SBU manager should be made visible across the company. An SBU manager is unlikely to surrender key people if only the other business (or the general manager of that business who may be a competitor for promotion) is going to benefit from the redeployment. Cooperative SBU managers should be celebrated as team players. Where priorities are clear, transfers are less likely to be seen as idiosyncratic and politically motivated.

Transfers for the sake of building core competence must be recorded and appreciated in the corporate memory. It is reasonable to expect a business that has surrendered core skills on behalf of corporate opportunities in other areas to lose, for a time, some of its competitiveness. If these losses in performance bring immediate censure, SBUs will be unlikely to assent to skills transfers next time.

Finally, there are ways to wean key employees off the idea that they belong in perpetuity to any particular business. Early in their careers, people may be exposed to a variety of businesses through a carefully planned rotation program. At Canon, critical people move regularly between the camera business and the copier business and between the copier business and the professional optical-products business. In mid-career, periodic assignments to cross-divisional project teams may be necessary, both for diffusing core competencies and for loosening the bonds that might tie an individual to one business even when brighter opportunities beckon elsewhere. Those who embody critical core competencies should know that their careers are tracked and guided by corporate human resource professionals. In the early 1980s at Canon, all engineers under 30 were invited to apply for membership on a seven-person committee that was to spend two years plotting Canon's future direction, including its strategic architecture.

Competence carriers should be regularly brought together from across the corporation to trade notes and ideas. The goal is to build a strong feeling of community among these people. To a great extent, their loyalty should be to the integrity of the core competence area they represent and not just to particular businesses. In traveling regularly, talking frequently to customers, and meeting with peers, competence carriers may be encouraged to discover new market opportunities.

Core competencies are the wellspring of new business development. They should constitute the focus for strategy at the corporate level. Managers have to win manufacturing leadership in core products and capture global share through brand-building programs aimed at exploiting economies of scope. Only if the company is conceived of as a hierarchy of core competencies, core products, and market-focused business units will it be fit to fight.

Nor can top management be just another layer of accounting consolidation, which it often is in a regime of radical decentralization. Top management must add value by enunciating the strategic architecture that guides the competence acquisition process. We believe an obsession with competence building will characterize the global winners of the 1990s. With the decade underway, the time for rethinking the concept of the corporation is already overdue.

Vickers Learns the Value of Strategic Architecture

THE IDEA THAT top management should develop a corporate strategy for acquiring and deploying core competencies is relatively new in most U.S. companies. There are a few exceptions. An early convert was Trinova (previously Libbey Owens Ford), a Toledo-based corporation, which enjoys a worldwide position in power and motion controls and engineered plastics. One of its major divisions is Vickers, a premier supplier of hydraulics components like valves, pumps, actuators, and filtration devices to aerospace, marine, defense, automotive, earth-moving, and industrial markets.

Vickers saw the potential for a transformation of its traditional business with the application of electronics disciplines in combination with its traditional technologies. The goal was "to ensure that change in technology does not displace Vickers from its customers." This, to be sure, was initially a defensive move: Vickers recognized that unless it acquired new skills, it could not protect existing markets or capitalize on new growth opportunities. Managers at Vickers attempted to conceptualize the likely evolution of (a) technologies relevant to the power and motion control business, (b) functionalities that would satisfy emerging customer needs, and (c) new competencies needed to creatively manage the marriage of technology and customer needs.

Despite pressure for short-term earnings, top management looked to a 10- to 15-year time horizon in developing a map of emerging customer needs, changing technologies, and the core competencies that would be necessary to bridge the gap between the two. Its slogan was "Into the 21st Century." (A simplified version of the overall architecture developed is shown here.) Vickers is currently in fluid-power components. The architecture identifies two additional competencies, electric-power components and electronic controls. A systems integration capability that would unite hardware, software, and service was also targeted for development.

The strategic architecture, as illustrated by the Vickers example, is not a forecast of specific products or specific technologies but a broad map of the evolving linkages between customer functionality requirements, potential technologies, and core competencies. It assumes that products and systems cannot be defined with certainty for the future but that preempting competitors in the development of new markets requires an early start to building core competencies. The strategic architecture developed by Vickers, while describing the future in competence terms, also provides the basis for making "here and now" decisions about product priorities, acquisitions, alliances, and recruitment.

Since 1986, Vickers has made more than ten clearly targeted acquisitions, each one focused on a specific component or technology gap identified in the overall architecture. The architecture is also the basis for internal development of new

Vickers Map of Competencies

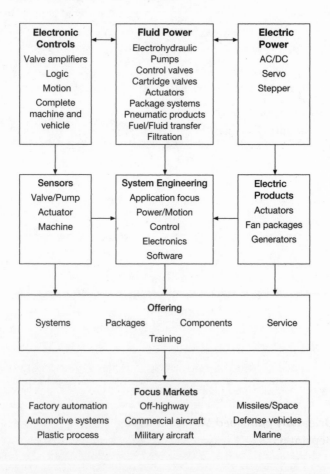

competencies. Vickers has undertaken, in parallel, a reorganization to enable the integration of electronics and electrical capabilities with mechanical-based competencies. We believe that it will take another two to three years before Vickers reaps the total benefits from developing the strategic architecture, communicating it widely to all its employees, customers, and investors, and building administrative systems consistent with the architecture.

Notes

1. For a fuller discussion, see our article, "Strategic Intent" HBR May–June 1989, p. 63.

2. "Collaborate with Your Competitors and Win," HBR January–February 1989, p. 133, with Yves L. Doz.

Originally published May–June 1990
Reprint 6528

Disruptive Technologies

Catching the Wave

JOSEPH L. BOWER AND
CLAYTON M. CHRISTENSEN

Executive Summary

ONE OF THE MOST CONSISTENT patterns in
business is the failure of leading companies to stay
at the top of their industries when technologies or
markets change. Why is it that established companies invest aggressively—and successfully—in the
technologies necessary to retain their current
customers but then fail to make the technological
investments that customers of the future will
demand? The fundamental reason is that leading
companies succumb to one of the most popular,
and valuable, management dogmas: they stay
close to their customers.

Customers wield extraordinary power in directing a company's investments. But what happens
when a new technology emerges that customers
reject because it *doesn't* address their needs as

effectively as a company's current approach? In an ongoing study of technological change, the authors found that most established companies are consistently ahead of their industries in developing and commercializing new technologies as long as those technologies address the next-generation-performance needs of their customers. However, an industry's leaders are rarely in the forefront of commercializing new technologies that don't initially meet the functional demands of mainstream customers and appeal only to small or emerging markets.

To remain at the top of their industries, managers must first be able to spot the technologies that fall into this category. To pursue these technologies, managers must protect them from the processes and incentives that are geared to serving mainstream customers. And the only way to do that is to create organizations that are completely independent of the mainstream business.

ONE OF THE MOST CONSISTENT patterns in business is the failure of leading companies to stay at the top of their industries when technologies or markets change. Goodyear and Firestone entered the radial-tire market quite late. Xerox let Canon create the small-copier market. Bucyrus-Erie allowed Caterpillar and Deere to take over the mechanical excavator market. Sears gave way to Wal-Mart.

The pattern of failure has been especially striking in the computer industry. IBM dominated the mainframe market but missed by years the emergence of minicomputers, which were technologically much simpler than mainframes. Digital Equipment dominated the mini-computer market with innovations like its VAX architecture but missed the personal-computer market almost completely. Apple Computer led the world of personal computing and established the standard for user-friendly computing but lagged five years behind the leaders in bringing its portable computer to market.

Why is it that companies like these invest aggressively—and successfully—in the technologies necessary to retain their current customers but then fail to make certain other technological investments that customers of the future will demand? Undoubtedly, bureaucracy, arrogance, tired executive blood, poor planning, and short-term investment horizons have all played a role. But a more fundamental reason lies at the heart of the paradox: leading companies succumb to one of the most popular, and valuable, management dogmas. They stay close to their customers.

Although most managers like to think they are in control, customers wield extraordinary power in directing a company's investments. Before managers decide to launch a technology, develop a product, build a plant, or establish new channels of distribution, they must look to their customers first: Do their customers want it? How big will the market be? Will the investment be profitable? The more astutely managers ask and answer these questions, the more completely their investments will be aligned with the needs of their customers.

This is the way a well-managed company should operate. Right? But what happens when customers reject a new technology, product concept, or way of doing business because it does not address their needs as effectively as a company's current approach? The large photocopying centers that represented the core of Xerox's customer base at first had no use for small, slow tabletop copiers. The excavation contractors that had relied on Bucyrus-Erie's big-bucket steam- and diesel-powered cable shovels didn't want hydraulic excavators because initially they were small and weak. IBM's large commercial, government, and industrial customers saw no immediate use for minicomputers. In each instance, companies listened to their customers, gave them the product performance they were looking for, and, in the end, were hurt by the very technologies their customers led them to ignore.

We have seen this pattern repeatedly in an on-going study of leading companies in a variety of industries that have confronted technological change. The research shows that most well-managed, established companies are consistently ahead of their industries in developing and commercializing new technologies—from incremental improvements to radically new approaches—as long as those technologies address the next-generation performance needs of their customers. However, these same companies are rarely in the forefront of commercializing new technologies that don't initially meet the needs of mainstream customers and appeal only to small or emerging markets.

Using the rational, analytical investment processes that most well-managed companies have developed, it is nearly impossible to build a cogent case for diverting resources from known customer needs in established markets to markets and customers that seem insignificant or do not yet exist. After all, meeting the needs of established customers and fending off competitors takes all the resources a company has, and then some. In well-managed companies, the processes used to identify customers' needs, forecast technological trends, assess profitability, allocate resources across competing proposals for investment, and take new products to market are focused—for all the right reasons—on current customers and markets. These processes are designed to weed out proposed products and technologies that do *not* address customers' needs.

In fact, the processes and incentives that companies use to keep focused on their main customers work so well that they blind those companies to important new technologies in emerging markets. Many companies have learned the hard way the perils of ignoring new technologies that do not initially meet the needs of mainstream customers. For example, although personal computers did not meet the requirements of mainstream minicomputer users in the early 1980s, the computing power of the desktop machines improved at a much faster rate than minicomputer users' *demands* for computing power did. As a result, personal computers caught up with the computing needs of many of the customers of Wang, Prime, Nixdorf, Data General, and Digital Equipment. Today they are performance-competitive with minicomputers in many applications. For the minicomputer makers, keeping close to mainstream customers and ignoring what were initially low-performance desktop technologies used by seemingly insignificant customers in emerging markets was a rational decision—but one that proved disastrous.

The technological changes that damage established companies are usually not radically new or difficult from a *technological* point of view. They do, however, have two important characteristics: First, they typically present a different package of performance attributes—ones that, at least at the outset, are not valued by existing customers. Second, the performance attributes that existing customers do value improve at such a rapid rate that the new technology can later invade those established markets. Only at this point will mainstream customers want the technology. Unfortunately for the established suppliers, by then it is often too late: the pioneers of the new technology dominate the market.

It follows, then, that senior executives must first be able to spot the technologies that seem to fall into this category. Next, to commercialize and develop the new technologies, managers must protect them from the processes and incentives that are geared to serving established customers. And the only way to protect them is to create organizations that are completely independent from the mainstream business.

No industry demonstrates the danger of staying too close to customers more dramatically than the hard-disk-drive industry. Between 1976 and 1992, disk-drive performance improved at a stunning rate: the physical size of a 100-megabyte (MB) system shrank from 5,400 to 8 cubic inches, and the cost per MB fell from $560 to $5. Technological change, of course, drove these breathtaking achievements. About half of the improvement came from a host of radical advances that were critical to continued improvements in disk-drive performance; the other half came from incremental advances.

The pattern in the disk-drive industry has been repeated in many other industries: the leading, established companies have consistently led the industry in developing and adopting new technologies that their customers demanded—even when those technologies required completely different technological competencies and manufacturing capabilities from the ones the companies had. In spite of this aggressive technological posture, no single disk-drive manufacturer has been able to dominate the industry for more than a few years. A series of companies have entered the business and risen to prominence, only to be toppled by newcomers who pursued technologies that at first did not meet the needs of mainstream customers. As a result, not one of the independent disk-drive companies that existed in 1976 survives today.

To explain the differences in the impact of certain kinds of technological innovations on a given industry, the concept of *performance trajectories*—the rate at which the performance of a product has improved, and is expected to improve, over time—can be helpful. Almost every industry has a critical performance trajectory. In mechanical excavators, the critical trajectory is the annual improvement in cubic yards of earth moved per minute. In photocopiers, an important performance trajectory is improvement in number of copies per minute. In disk drives, one crucial measure of performance is storage capacity, which has advanced 50% each year on average for a given size of drive.

Different types of technological innovations affect performance trajectories in different ways. On the one hand, *sustaining* technologies tend to maintain a rate of improvement; that is, they give customers something more or better in the attributes they already value. For example, thin-film components in disk drives, which replaced conventional ferrite heads and oxide disks between 1982 and 1990, enabled information to be recorded more densely on disks. Engineers had been pushing the limits of the performance they could wring from ferrite heads and oxide disks, but the drives employing these technologies seemed to have reached the natural limits of an S curve. At that point, new thin film technologies emerged that restored—or sustained—the historical trajectory of performance improvement.

On the other hand, *disruptive* technologies introduce a very different package of attributes from the one mainstream customers historically value, and they often perform far worse along one or two dimensions that are particularly important to those customers. As a rule, mainstream customers are unwilling to use a disruptive product in applications they know and understand. At first, then, disruptive technologies tend to be used and valued only in new markets or new applications; in fact, they generally make possible the emergence of new markets. For example, Sony's early transistor radios sacrificed sound fidelity but created a market for portable radios by offering a new and different package of attributes—small size, light weight, and portability.

In the history of the hard-disk-drive industry, the leaders stumbled at each point of disruptive technological change: when the diameter of disk drives shrank from the original 14 inches to 8 inches, then to 5.25 inches, and finally to 3.5 inches. Each of these new architectures initially offered the market substantially less storage capacity than the typical user in the established market required. For example, the 8-inch drive offered 20 MB when it was introduced, while the primary market for disk drives at that time—mainframes—required 200 MB on average. Not surprisingly, the leading computer manufacturers rejected the 8-inch architecture at first. As a result, their suppliers, whose mainstream products consisted of 14-inch drives with more than 200 MB of capacity, did not pursue the disruptive products aggressively. The pattern was repeated when the 5.25-inch and 3.5-inch drives emerged: established computer makers rejected the drives as inadequate, and, in turn, their disk-drive suppliers ignored them as well.

But while they offered less storage capacity, the disruptive architectures created other important attributes—internal power supplies and smaller size (8-inch drives); still smaller size and low-cost stepper motors (5.25-inch drives); and ruggedness, light weight, and low-power consumption (3.5-inch drives). From the late 1970s to the mid-1980s, the availability of the three drives made possible the development of new markets for minicomputers, desktop PCs, and portable computers, respectively.

Although the smaller drives represented disruptive technological change, each was technologically straightforward. In fact, there were engineers at many leading companies who championed the new technologies and built working prototypes with bootlegged resources before management gave a formal go-ahead. Still, the leading companies could not move the products through their organizations and into the market in a timely way. Each time a disruptive technology emerged, between one-half and two-thirds of the established manufacturers failed to introduce models employing the new architecture—in stark contrast to their timely launches of critical sustaining technologies. Those companies that finally did launch new models typically lagged behind entrant companies by two years—eons in an industry whose products' life cycles are often two years. Three waves of entrant companies led these revolutions; they first captured the new markets and then dethroned the leading companies in the mainstream markets.

How could technologies that were initially inferior and useful only to new markets eventually threaten leading companies in established markets? Once the disruptive architectures became established in their new markets, sustaining innovations raised each architecture's performance along steep trajectories—so steep that the performance available from each architecture soon satisfied the needs of customers in the established markets. For example, the 5.25-inch drive, whose initial 5 MB of capacity in 1980 was only a fraction of the capacity that the minicomputer market needed, became fully performance-competitive in the minicomputer market by 1986 and in the mainframe market by 1991. (See the graph "How Disk-Drive Performance Met Market Needs.")

How Disk-Drive Performance Met Market Needs

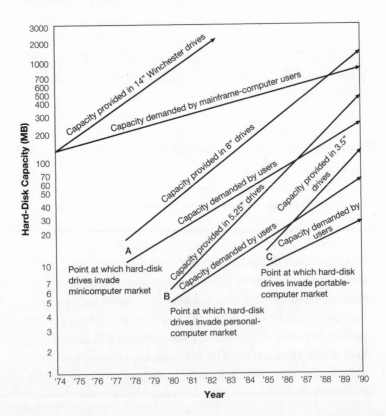

A company's revenue and cost structures play a critical role in the way it evaluates proposed technological innovations. Generally, disruptive technologies look financially unattractive to established companies. The potential revenues from the discernible markets are small, and it is often difficult to project how big the markets for the technology will be over the long term. As a result, managers typically conclude that the technology cannot make a meaningful contribution to corporate growth and, therefore, that it is not worth the management effort required to develop it. In addition, established companies have often installed higher cost structures to serve sustaining technologies than those required by disruptive technologies. As a result, managers typically see themselves as having two choices when deciding whether to pursue disruptive technologies. One is to go *downmarket* and accept the lower profit margins of the emerging markets that the disruptive technologies will initially serve. The other is to go *upmarket* with sustaining technologies and enter market segments whose profit margins are alluringly high. (For example, the margins of IBM's mainframes are still higher than those of PCs). Any rational resource-allocation process in companies serving established markets will choose going upmarket rather than going down.

Managers of companies that have championed disruptive technologies in emerging markets look at the world quite differently. Without the high cost structures of their established counterparts, these companies find the emerging markets appealing. Once the companies have secured a foothold in the markets and improved the performance of their technologies, the established markets above them, served by high-cost suppliers, look appetizing. When they do attack, the entrant companies find the established players to be easy and unprepared opponents because the opponents have been looking upmarket themselves, discounting the threat from below.

It is tempting to stop at this point and conclude that a valuable lesson has been learned: managers can avoid missing the next wave by paying careful attention to potentially disruptive technologies that do *not* meet current customers' needs. But recognizing the pattern and figuring out how to break it are two different things. Although entrants invaded established markets with new technologies three times in succession, none of the established leaders in the disk-drive industry seemed to learn from the experiences of those that fell before them. Management myopia or lack of foresight cannot explain these failures. The problem is that managers keep doing what has worked in the past: serving the rapidly growing needs of their current customers. The processes that successful, well-managed companies have developed to allocate resources among proposed investments are *incapable* of funneling resources into programs that current customers explicitly don't want and whose profit margins seem unattractive.

Managing the development of new technology is tightly linked to a company's investment processes. Most strategic proposals—to add capacity or to develop new products or processes—take shape at the lower levels of organizations in engineering groups or project teams. Companies then use analytical planning and budgeting systems to select from among the candidates competing for funds. Proposals to create new businesses in emerging markets are particularly challenging to assess because they depend on notoriously unreliable estimates of market size. Because managers are evaluated on their ability to place the right bets, it is not surprising that in well-managed companies, mid- and top-level managers back projects in which the market seems assured. By staying close to lead customers, as they have been trained to do, managers focus resources on fulfilling the requirements of those reliable customers that can be served profitably. Risk is reduced—and careers are safe-guarded—by giving known customers what they want.

Seagate Technology's experience illustrates the consequences of relying on such resource-allocation processes to evaluate disruptive technologies. By almost any measure, Seagate, based in Scotts Valley, California, was one of the most successful and aggressively managed companies in the history of the microelectronics industry: from its inception in 1980, Seagate's revenues had grown to more than $700 million by 1986. It had pioneered 5.25-inch hard-disk drives and was the main supplier of them to IBM and IBM-compatible personal-computer manufacturers. The company was the leading manufacturer of 5.25-inch drives at the time the disruptive 3.5-inch drives emerged in the mid-1980s.

Engineers at Seagate were the second in the industry to develop working prototypes of 3.5-inch drives. By early 1985, they had made more than 80 such models with a low level of company funding. The engineers forwarded the new models to key marketing executives, and the trade press reported that Seagate was actively developing 3.5-inch drives. But Seagate's principal customers—IBM and other manufacturers of AT-class personal computers—showed no interest in the new drives. They wanted to incorporate 40-MB and 60-MB drives in their next-generation models, and Seagate's early 3.5-inch prototypes packed only 10 MB. In response, Seagate's marketing executives lowered their sales forecasts for the new disk drives.

Manufacturing and financial executives at the company pointed out another drawback to the 3.5-inch drives. According to their analysis, the new drives would never be competitive with the 5.25-inch architecture on a cost-per-megabyte basis—an important metric that Seagate's customers used to evaluate disk drives. Given Seagate's cost structure, margins on the higher-capacity 5.25-inch models therefore promised to be much higher than those on the smaller products.

Senior managers quite rationally decided that the 3.5-inch drive would not provide the sales volume and profit margins that Seagate needed from a new product. A former Seagate marketing executive recalled, "We needed a new model that could become the next ST412 [a 5.25-inch drive generating more than $300 million in annual sales, which was nearing the end of its life cycle]. At the time, the entire market for 3.5-inch drives was less than $50 million. The 3.5-inch drive just didn't fit the bill—for sales or profits."

The shelving of the 3.5-inch drive was *not* a signal that Seagate was complacent about innovation. Seagate subsequently introduced new models of 5.25-inch drives at an accelerated rate and, in so doing, introduced an impressive array of sustaining technological improvements, even though introducing them rendered a significant portion of its manufacturing capacity obsolete.

While Seagate's attention was glued to the personal-computer market, former employees of Seagate and other 5.25-inch drive makers, who had become frustrated by their employers' delays in launching 3.5-inch drives, founded a new company, Conner Peripherals. Conner focused on selling its 3.5-inch drives to companies in emerging markets for portable computers and small-footprint desktop products (PCs that take up a smaller amount of space on a desk). Conner's primary customer was Compaq Computer, a customer that Seagate had never served. Seagate's own prosperity, coupled with Conner's focus on customers who valued different disk-drive attributes (ruggedness, physical volume, and weight), minimized the threat Seagate saw in Conner and its 3.5-inch drives.

From its beachhead in the emerging market for portable computers, however, Conner improved the storage capacity of its drives by 50% per year. By the end of 1987, 3.5-inch drives packed the capacity demanded in the mainstream personal-computer market. At this point, Seagate executives took their company's 3.5-inch drive off the shelf, introducing it to the market as a *defensive* response to the attack of entrant companies like Conner and Quantum Corporation, the other pioneer of 3.5-inch drives. But it was too late.

By then, Seagate faced strong competition. For a while, the company was able to defend its existing market by selling 3.5-inch drives to its established customer base—manufacturers and resellers of full-size personal computers. In fact, a large proportion of its 3.5-inch products continued to be shipped in frames that enabled its customers to mount the drives in computers designed to accommodate 5.25-inch drives. But, in the end, Seagate could only struggle to become a second-tier supplier in the new portable-computer market.

In contrast, Conner and Quantum built a dominant position in the new portable-computer market and then used their scale and experience base in designing and manufacturing 3.5-inch products to drive Seagate from the personal-computer market. In their 1994 fiscal years, the combined revenues of Conner and Quantum exceeded $5 billion.

Seagate's poor timing typifies the responses of many established companies to the emergence of disruptive technologies. Seagate was willing to enter the market for 3.5-inch drives only when it had become large enough to satisfy the company's financial requirements—that is, only when existing customers wanted the new technology. Seagate has survived through its savvy acquisition of Control Data Corporation's disk-drive business in 1990. With CDC's technology base and Seagate's volume-manufacturing expertise, the company has become a powerful player in the business of supplying large-capacity drives for high-end computers. Nonetheless, Seagate has been reduced to a shadow of its former self in the personal-computer market.

It should come as no surprise that few companies, when confronted with disruptive technologies, have been able to overcome the handicaps of size or success. But it can be done. There is a method to spotting and cultivating disruptive technologies.

DETERMINE WHETHER THE TECHNOLOGY IS DISRUPTIVE OR SUSTAINING

The first step is to decide which of the myriad technologies on the horizon are disruptive and, of those, which are real threats. Most companies have well-conceived processes for identifying and tracking the progress of potentially sustaining technologies, because they are important to serving and protecting current customers. But few have systematic processes in place to identify and track potentially disruptive technologies.

One approach to identifying disruptive technologies is to examine internal disagreements over the development of new products or technologies. Who supports the project and who doesn't? Marketing and financial managers, because of their managerial and financial incentives, will rarely support a disruptive technology. On the other hand, technical personnel with outstanding track records will often persist in arguing that a new market for the technology will emerge—even in the face of opposition from key customers and marketing and financial staff. Disagreement between the two groups often signals a disruptive technology that top-level managers should explore.

DEFINE THE STRATEGIC SIGNIFICANCE OF THE DISRUPTIVE TECHNOLOGY

The next step is to ask the right people the right questions about the strategic importance of the disruptive technology. Disruptive technologies tend to stall early in strategic reviews because managers either ask the wrong questions or ask the wrong people the right questions. For example, established companies have regular procedures for asking mainstream customers—especially the important accounts where new ideas are actually tested—to assess the value of innovative products. Generally, these customers are selected because they are the ones striving the hardest to stay ahead of *their* competitors in pushing the performance of *their* products. Hence these customers are most likely to demand the highest performance from their suppliers. For this reason, lead customers are reliably accurate when it comes to assessing the potential of sustaining technologies, but they are reliably *in*accurate when it comes to assessing the potential of disruptive technologies. They are the wrong people to ask.

A simple graph plotting product performance as it is defined in mainstream markets on the vertical axis and time on the horizontal axis can help managers identify both the right questions and the right people to ask.

First, draw a line depicting the level of performance and the trajectory of performance improvement that customers have historically enjoyed and are likely to expect in the future. Then locate the estimated initial performance level of the new technology. If the technology is disruptive, the point will lie far below the performance demanded by current customers. (See the graph "How to Assess Disruptive Technologies.")

What is the likely slope of performance improvement of the disruptive technology compared with the slope of performance improvement demanded by existing markets? If knowledgeable technologists believe the new technology might progress faster than the market's demand for performance improvement, then that technology, which does not meet customers' needs today, may very well address them tomorrow. The new technology, therefore, is strategically critical.

How to Assess Disruptive Technologies

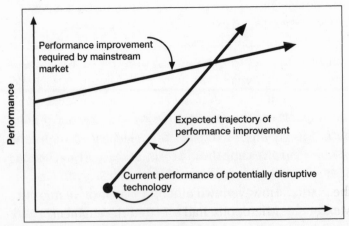

Instead of taking this approach, most managers ask the wrong questions. They compare the anticipated rate of performance improvement of the new technology with that of the established technology. If the new technology has the potential to surpass the established one, the reasoning goes, they should get busy developing it.

Pretty simple. But this sort of comparison, while valid for sustaining technologies, misses the central strategic issue in assessing potentially disruptive technologies. Many of the disruptive technologies we studied *never* surpassed the capability of the old technology. It is the trajectory of the disruptive technology compared with that of the *market* that is significant. For example, the reason the mainframe-computer market is shrinking is not that personal computers outperform mainframes but because personal computers networked with a file server meet the computing and data-storage needs of many organizations effectively. Mainframe-computer makers are reeling not because the performance of personal-computing technology surpassed the performance of mainframe *technology* but because it intersected with the performance demanded by the established *market*.

Consider the graph again. If technologists believe that the new technology will progress at the same rate as the market's demand for performance improvement, the disruptive technology may be slower to invade established markets. Recall that Seagate had targeted personal computing, where demand for hard-disk capacity per computer was growing at 30% per year. Because the capacity of 3.5-inch drives improved at a much faster rate, leading 3.5-inch-drive makers were able to force Seagate out of the market. However, two other 5.25-inch-drive makers, Maxtor and Micropolis, had targeted the engineering-workstation market, in which demand for hard-disk capacity was insatiable. In that market, the trajectory of capacity demanded was essentially parallel to the trajectory of capacity improvement that technologists could supply in the 3.5-inch architecture. As a result, entering the 3.5-inch-drive business was strategically less critical for those companies than it was for Seagate.

LOCATE THE INITIAL MARKET FOR THE DISRUPTIVE TECHNOLOGY

Once managers have determined that a new technology is disruptive and strategically critical, the next step is to locate the initial markets for that technology. Market research, the tool that managers have traditionally relied on, is seldom helpful: at the point a company needs to make a strategic commitment to a disruptive technology, no concrete market exists. When Edwin Land asked Polaroid's market researchers to assess the potential sales of his new camera, they concluded that Polaroid would sell a mere 100,000 cameras over the product's lifetime; few people they interviewed could imagine the uses of instant photography.

Because disruptive technologies frequently signal the emergence of new markets or market segments, managers must *create* information about such markets—who the customers will be, which dimensions of product performance will matter most to which customers, what the right price points will be. Managers can create this kind of information only by experimenting rapidly, iteratively, and inexpensively with both the product and the market.

For established companies to undertake such experiments is very difficult. The resource-allocation processes that are critical to profitability and competitiveness will not—and should not—direct resources to markets in which sales will be relatively small. How, then, can an established company probe a market for a disruptive technology? Let start-ups—either ones the company funds or others with no connection to the company—conduct the experiments. Small, hungry organizations are good at placing economical bets, rolling with the punches, and agilely changing product and market strategies in response to feedback from initial forays into the market.

Consider Apple Computer in its start-up days. The company's original product, the Apple I, was a flop when it was launched in 1977. But Apple had not placed a huge bet on the product and had gotten at least *something* into the hands of early users quickly. The company learned a lot from the Apple I about the new technology and about what customers wanted and did not want. Just as important, a group of customers learned about what they did and did not want from personal computers. Armed with this information, Apple launched the Apple II quite successfully.

Many companies could have learned the same valuable lessons by watching Apple closely. In fact, some companies pursue an explicit strategy of being *second to invent*—allowing small pioneers to lead the way into uncharted market territory. For instance, IBM let Apple, Commodore, and Tandy define the personal computer. It then aggressively entered the market and built a considerable personal-computer business.

But IBM's relative success in entering a new market late is the exception, not the rule. All too often, successful companies hold the performance of small-market pioneers to the financial standards they apply to their own performance. In an attempt to ensure that they are using their resources well, companies explicitly or implicitly set relatively high thresholds for the size of the markets they should consider entering. This approach sentences them to making late entries into markets already filled with powerful players.

For example, when the 3.5-inch drive emerged, Seagate needed a $300-million-a-year product to replace its mature flagship 5.25-inch model, the ST412, and the 3.5-inch market wasn't large enough. Over the next two years, when the trade press asked when Seagate would introduce its 3.5-inch drive, company executives consistently responded that there was no market yet. There actually *was* a market, and it was growing rapidly. The signals that Seagate was picking up about the market, influenced as they were by customers who didn't want 3.5-inch drives, were misleading. When Seagate finally introduced its 3.5-inch drive in 1987, more than $750 million in 3.5-inch drives had already been sold. Information about the market's size had been widely available throughout the industry. But it wasn't compelling enough to shift the focus of Seagate's managers. They continued to look at the new market through the eyes of their current customers and in the context of their current financial structure.

The posture of today's leading disk-drive makers toward the newest disruptive technology, 1.8-inch drives, is eerily familiar. Each of the industry leaders has designed one or more models of the tiny drives, and the models are sitting on shelves. Their capacity is too low to be used in notebook computers, and no one yet knows where the initial market for 1.8-inch drives will be. Fax machines, printers, and automobile dashboard mapping systems are all candidates. "There just isn't a market," complained one industry executive. "We've got the

product, and the sales force can take orders for it. But
there are no orders because nobody needs it. It just sits
there." This executive has not considered the fact that
his sales force has no incentive to sell the 1.8-inch drives
instead of the higher-margin products it sells to higher-
volume customers. And while the 1.8-inch drive is sitting
on the shelf at his company and others, last year more
than $50 million worth of 1.8-inch drives were sold,
almost all by start-ups. This year, the market will be an
estimated $150 million.

To avoid allowing small, pioneering companies to
dominate new markets, executives must personally mon-
itor the available intelligence on the progress of pioneering companies through monthly meetings with
technologists, academics, venture capitalists, and other
nontraditional sources of information. They *cannot* rely
on the company's traditional channels for gauging markets because those channels were not designed for that
purpose.

PLACE RESPONSIBILITY FOR BUILDING A DISRUPTIVE-TECHNOLOGY BUSINESS IN AN INDEPENDENT ORGANIZATION

The strategy of forming small teams into skunk-works
projects to isolate them from the stifling demands of
mainstream organizations is widely known but poorly
understood. For example, isolating a team of engineers
so that it can develop a radically new sustaining technology just because that technology is radically different is a
fundamental misapplication of the skunk-works
approach. Managing out of context is also unnecessary
in the unusual event that a disruptive technology is more
financially attractive than existing products. Consider

Intel's transition from dynamic random access memory (DRAM) chips to microprocessors. Intel's early microprocessor business had a higher gross margin than that of its DRAM business; in other words, Intel's normal resource-allocation process naturally provided the new business with the resources it needed.[1]

Creating a separate organization is necessary only when the disruptive technology has a lower profit margin than the mainstream business and must serve the unique needs of a new set of customers. CDC, for example, successfully created a remote organization to commercialize its 5.25-inch drive. Through 1980, CDC was the dominant independent disk-drive supplier due to its expertise in making 14-inch drives for mainframe-computer makers. When the 8-inch drive emerged, CDC launched a late development effort, but its engineers were repeatedly pulled off the project to solve problems for the more profitable, higher-priority 14-inch projects targeted at the company's most important customers. As a result, CDC was three years late in launching its first 8-inch product and never captured more than 5% of that market.

When the 5.25-inch generation arrived, CDC decided that it would face the new challenge more strategically. The company assigned a small group of engineers and marketers in Oklahoma City, Oklahoma, far from the mainstream organization's customers, the task of developing and commercializing a competitive 5.25-inch product. "We needed to launch it in an environment in which everybody got excited about a $50,000 order," one executive recalled. "In Minneapolis, you needed a $1 million order to turn anyone's head." CDC never regained the 70% share it had once enjoyed in the market for mainframe disk drives, but its Oklahoma City operation secured a profitable 20% of the high-performance 5.25-inch market.

Had Apple created a similar organization to develop its Newton personal digital assistant (PDA), those who have pronounced it a flop might have deemed it a success. In launching the product, Apple made the mistake of acting as if it were dealing with an established market. Apple managers went into the PDA project assuming that it had to make a significant contribution to corporate growth. Accordingly, they researched customer desires exhaustively and then bet huge sums launching the Newton. Had Apple made a more modest technological and financial bet and entrusted the Newton to an organization the size that Apple itself was when it launched the Apple I, the outcome might have been different. The Newton might have been seen more broadly as a solid step forward in the quest to discover what customers really want. In fact, many more Newtons than Apple I models were sold within a year of their introduction.

KEEP THE DISRUPTIVE ORGANIZATION INDEPENDENT

Established companies can only dominate emerging markets by creating small organizations of the sort CDC created in Oklahoma City. But what should they do when the emerging market becomes large and established?

Most managers assume that once a spin-off has become commercially viable in a new market, it should be integrated into the mainstream organization. They reason that the fixed costs associated with engineering, manufacturing, sales, and distribution activities can be shared across a broader group of customers and products.

This approach might work with sustaining technologies; however, with disruptive technologies, folding the spin-off into the mainstream organization can be disastrous. When the independent and mainstream organizations are folded together in order to share resources, debilitating arguments inevitably arise over which groups get what resources and whether or when to cannibalize established products. In the history of the disk-drive industry, *every* company that has tried to manage mainstream and disruptive businesses within a single organization failed.

No matter the industry, a corporation consists of business units with finite life spans: the technological and market bases of any business will eventually disappear. Disruptive technologies are part of that cycle. Companies that understand this process can create new businesses to replace the ones that must inevitably die. To do so, companies must give managers of disruptive innovation free rein to realize the technology's full potential—even if it means ultimately killing the mainstream business. For the corporation to live, it must be willing to see business units die. If the corporation doesn't kill them off itself, competitors will.

The key to prospering at points of disruptive change is not simply to take more risks, invest for the long term, or fight bureaucracy. The key is to manage strategically important disruptive technologies in an organizational context where small orders create energy, where fast low-cost forays into ill-defined markets are possible, and where overhead is low enough to permit profit even in emerging markets.

Managers of established companies can master disruptive technologies with extraordinary success. But when they seek to develop and launch a disruptive technology that is rejected by important customers within the context of the mainstream business's financial demands, they fail—not because they make the wrong decisions, but because they make the right decisions for circumstances that are about to become history.

Notes

1. Robert A. Burgelman, "Fading Memories: A Process Theory of Strategic Business Exit in Dynamic Environments," *Administrative Science Quarterly* 39 (1994), pp. 24–56.

Originally published January–February 1995
Reprint 3510

Regional Strategies for Global Leadership

PANKAJ GHEMAWAT

Executive Summary

THE LEADERS OF such global powerhouses as
GE, Wal-Mart, and Toyota seem to have grasped
two crucial truths: First, far from becoming submerged by the rising tide of globalization, geographic and other regional distinctions may in fact
be increasing in importance. Second, regionally
focused strategies, used in conjunction with local
and global initiatives, can significantly boost a
company's performance.

The business and economic data reveal a highly
rationalized world. For example, trade within
regions, rather than across them, drove the surge
of international commerce in the second half of
the twentieth century. Regionalization is also
apparent in foreign direct investment, companies'

197

international sales, and competition among the world's largest multinationals.

Harvard Business School professor Pankaj Ghemawat says that the most successful companies employ five types of regional strategies in addition to—or even instead of—global ones: home base, portfolio, hub, platform, and mandate. Some companies adopt the strategies in sequence, but the most nimble switch from one to another and combine approaches as their markets and businesses evolve. At Toyota, for example, exports from the home base continue to be substantial even as the company builds up an international manufacturing presence. And as Toyota achieves economies of scale and scope with a strong network of hubs, the company also pursues economies of specialization through interregional mandates.

Embracing regional strategies requires flexibility and creativity. A company must decide what constitutes a region, choose the most appropriate strategies, and mesh those strategies with the organization's existing structures. In a world that is neither truly global nor truly local, finding ways of coordinating within and across regions can deliver a powerful competitive advantage.

LET'S ASSUME THAT YOUR FIRM has a significant international presence. In that case, it probably has something called a "global strategy," which almost certainly represents an extraordinary investment of time, money, and energy. You and your colleagues may have adopted it with great fanfare. But, quite possibly, it has proven less than satisfactory as a road map to cross-border competition.

Disappointment with strategies that operate at a global level may explain why companies that do perform well internationally apply a regionally oriented strategy in addition to—or even instead of—a global one. Put differently, global as well as regional companies need to think through strategy at the regional level.

Jeffrey Immelt, CEO of GE, claims that regional teams are the key to his company's globalization initiatives, and he has moved to graft a network of regional headquarters onto GE's otherwise lean product-division structure. John Menzer, president and CEO of Wal-Mart International, tells employees that global leverage is about playing 3-d chess—at the global, regional, and local levels. Toyota may have gone furthest in exploiting the power of regionalized thinking. As Vice Chairman Fujio Cho says, "We intend to continue moving forward with globalization . . . by further enhancing the localization and independence of our operations in each region."

The leaders of these successful companies seem to have grasped two important truths about the global economy. First, geographic and other distinctions haven't been submerged by the rising tide of globalization; in fact, such distinctions are arguably increasing in importance. Second, regionally focused strategies are not just a halfway house between local (country-focused) and global strategies but a discrete family of strategies that, used in conjunction with local and global initiatives, can significantly boost a company's performance.

In the following article, I'll describe the various regional strategies successful companies have employed, showing how they have switched among the strategies and combined them as their markets and businesses have evolved. I'll begin, though, by looking more closely at the economic reasons why regions are often a critical unit of analysis for cross-border strategies.

The Reality of Regions

The most common pitch for taking regions seriously is that the emergence of regional blocs has stalled the process of globalization. Implicit in this view is a tendency to see regionalization as an alternative to further cross-border economic integration.

In fact, a close look at the country-level numbers suggests that increasing cross-border integration has been accompanied by high or rising levels of regionalization. In other words, regions are not an impediment to but an enabler of cross-border integration. As the exhibit "Trade: Regional or Global?" shows, the surge of trade in the second half of the twentieth century was driven more by activity within regions than across regions. The numbers also cast doubt on the idea (held implicitly by advocates of pure global strategies) that economic vitality is promoted more by cross-regional trade. It turns out that regions whose internal trade flows are the lowest relative to trade flows with other regions—Africa, the Middle East, and some of the Eastern European transition economies—are also the poorest economic performers.

Country-level numbers also suggest that foreign direct investment (FDI) is quite regionalized, which is even more surprising than the regionalization of trade. Data from the United Nations Conference on Trade and Development show that for the two dozen countries that account for nearly 90% of the world's outward FDI stock, the median share of intraregional FDI in total FDI was 52% in 2002, the most recent year for which data are available.

The extent and persistence of regionalization in economic activity reflect the continuing importance not only of geographic proximity but also of cultural, administrative, and, to some extent, economic proximity.[1] These four factors are interrelated: Countries that are relatively close to one another are also likely to share commonalities along the other dimensions. What's more, those similarities have intensified in the past few decades through free trade agreements, regional trade

---

Trade: Regional or Global?

In many parts of the world, intraregional trade increased steadily as a percentage of a region's total trade in the second half of the twentieth century. For example, in 1958 some 35% of trade in Asia and Oceania took place between countries in that geographic region. In 2000, the proportion was more than 50%. Globally, the proportion of trade within regions rose from about 47% to 55% between 1958 and 2000. The only significant decline has been in Eastern Europe, but that is explained by the collapse of communism. In general, the numbers indicate that increasing economic integration through international trade has been accompanied by increasing rather than decreasing regionalization.

Intraregional Trade as a Percentage of Total Trade

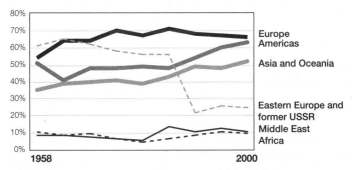

Source: United Nations, *International Trade Statistics Yearbooks*, 1958 to 2000.

preferences and tax treaties, and even currency unifica-
tion, with NAFTA and the European Union supplying
the two most obvious examples. Ironically, some differences between countries within a region can combine
with the similarities to expand the region's overall economic activity. For instance, we see U.S. firms in many
industries nearshoring production facilities to Mexico,
thereby arbitraging across economic differences between
the two countries while retaining the advantages of geographic proximity and administrative and political similarities, which more distant countries, such as China, do
not enjoy.

Evidence from companies' international sales also
points to considerable regionalization. According to data
analyzed by Susan Feinberg at Rutgers Business School,
among U.S. companies operating in only one foreign
country, there is a 60% chance that the country is
Canada. Even the largest multinational corporations
exhibit a significant regional bias. A study published by
Alan Rugman and Alain Verbeke in the *Journal of International Business Studies* shows that around 88% of the
world's biggest multinationals derive at least 50% of their
sales—the weighted average is 80%—from their home
regions. Just 2% (a total of nine companies) derive 20%
or more of their sales from each of the triad of North
America, Europe, and Asia.

Zooming in on large companies with relatively broad
regional footprints—roughly akin to the top 12% of the
previous sample—we find that even here competitive
interactions are often regionally focused. Take the case of
the aluminum-smelting industry. As we see in the exhibit
"Industry: Regional or Global?" in the last ten years the
industry has experienced some increase in concentration
as measured by the Herfindahl index (a standard measure

of industry concentration; the higher the index, the larger the market shares of the largest firms). But that increase in concentration reverses less than one-half of the decline of the previous 20 years, or about one-tenth of the decline experienced since 1950. In contrast, concentration in North America has doubled in the last ten years after holding more or less steady for the previous 20 years. Similar patterns appear in a range of other industries: personal computers, beer, and cement, to name just

---

Industry: Regional or Global?

In many "global" industries, competition is playing out at a regional level. The chart below measures concentration in the aluminum-smelting industry as a summary measure of the distribution of market shares within it. The metric used is the Herfindahl index, which measures the degree to which the industry is fragmented (lots of small to medium-sized companies splitting most of the business) or concentrated (a few players controlling most of the business). The higher the index, the larger the market shares of the largest companies. As the chart shows, the level of global competition was relatively flat from 1975 to 2000, while concentration in North America over the same period increased dramatically.

Concentration in the Aluminum-Smelting Industry

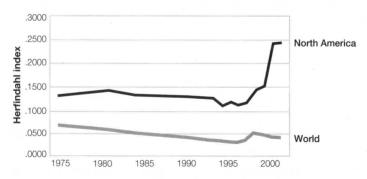

Source: Fariborz Ghadar, Center for Global Business Studies, Penn State University.

three. In other words, regions are often the level at which global oligopolists try to build up powerhouse positions.

Let's now take a closer look at the menu of regional strategies from which your company can choose.

The Regional Strategy Menu

Broadly speaking, regional strategies can be classified into five types, each with distinct strengths and weaknesses. I have ordered the strategies according to their relative complexity, starting with the simplest, but that does not mean companies necessarily progress through the strategies as they evolve. Whereas some companies may indeed adopt the strategies in the order in which I present them, others may find themselves abandoning more-advanced strategies in favor of simpler ones—good business is about striving to maximize value, not complexity. And capable companies will often use elements of several strategies simultaneously.

THE HOME BASE STRATEGY

Except for the very few companies that are virtually born global, such as Indian software services firms, companies generally start their international expansion by serving nearby foreign markets from their home base, locating all their R&D and, usually, manufacturing in their country of origin. The home base is also where the bulk of the *Fortune* Global 500 still focuses. Even companies that have since moved on to more complex regional strategies nonetheless rely on a home base strategy—at the regional level—for long periods. Thus, for decades, Toyota's international sales came exclusively from direct exports. And some companies that move on eventually return to a home base strategy: GE did so in home appliances, as did Bayer in pharmaceuticals.

For other companies, however, a focus on the home region is a matter of neither default nor devolution but, instead, the desired long-term strategy. Take the case of Zara, the Spanish fashion company. In a cycle that takes between two and four weeks, Zara designs and makes items near its manufacturing and logistics hub in northwestern Spain and trucks those goods to Western European markets. This rapid response lets the company produce what is selling during a fashion season instead of committing to merchandise before the season starts. The enhanced customer appeal and reduced incidence of markdowns have so far more than offset the extra costs of producing in Europe instead of Asia.

As Zara illustrates, home base strategies work well when the economics of concentration outweigh the economics of dispersion. Fashion-sensitive items do not travel easily from the Spanish hub to other regions, because the costs of expedited air shipments compromise the company's low-price positioning. More generally, the presence of any factor that collapses distance *within* the local region (such as regional grids in energy) will encourage companies to favor a single-region, home base strategy.

For some companies, the "region" that can be served from the home base is actually the globe. Operating in the highly globalized memory chip business, the Korean giant Samsung has one of the most balanced worldwide sales distributions of any major business, but it considers the colocation of most R&D and production at one site in South Korea to be a key competitive advantage. Transport costs are so low relative to product value that geographic concentration—which permits rapid

interactions and iteration across R&D and production—
dominates geographic dispersion even at the global level.

But cases like Samsung are rare. Typically, doing business from the home base effectively limits a company to
its local region. As a result, the biggest threats to companies pursuing a home base strategy are running out of
room to grow or failing to hedge risk adequately. Growth
within Europe will soon be an issue for Zara. And risk has
already emerged as a major concern: As of this writing,
the sharp decline of the dollar against the euro has
inflated Zara's costs of production relative to competitors
that rely more on dollar-denominated imports from Asia.

THE PORTFOLIO STRATEGY

This strategy involves setting up or acquiring operations
outside the home region that report directly to the home
base. It is usually the first strategy adopted by companies
seeking to establish a presence outside the markets they
can serve from home. The advantages of this approach
include faster growth in nonhome regions, significant
home positions that generate large amounts of cash, and
the opportunity to average out economic shocks and
cycles across regions.

A good example of a successful portfolio strategy is
provided by Toyota's initial investments in the United
States, which seemed tied together by little more than
the desire to build up a manufacturing presence in the
company's most important overseas market. What pre-
vented this approach from destroying value was Toyota's
distinct competitive advantage: the celebrated Toyota
Production System (TPS), which was developed and still
works best at home in Japan but could be applied to fac-
tories in the United States.

Although the portfolio strategy is conceptually simple, it takes time to implement, especially if a company tries to expand organically. It took Toyota more than a decade to establish itself in North America—a process that began with a joint venture with General Motors in the early 1980s. For an automaker lacking an advantage like TPS, the organic buildup of a significant presence in a new region could take far longer. Of course, companies may build a regional portfolio more quickly through acquisitions, but even that can take a decade or more. When Jack Welch began GE's globalization initiative in the second half of the 1980s, he targeted expansion in Europe, giving a trusted confidant, Nani Beccalli, wide latitude for deal making. Thanks to Beccalli's acquisitions, GE built up a strong presence in Europe, but the process of assembling the regional portfolio lasted until the early 2000s.

Companies that adopt a portfolio strategy often struggle to deal with rivals in nonhome regions. That's largely because portfolio strategies offer limited scope for letting regional—as opposed to local or global—considerations influence what happens on the ground at the local level. Indeed, this was precisely the experience of GE, whose European businesses reported to the global headquarters in the United States, run by purported "global leaders"—many of whom were Americans who had never lived or worked abroad. Meanwhile, most of GE's toughest competitors in its nonfinancial businesses were European companies that knew their increasingly regionalized home turf and were prepared to compete aggressively there. During a talk at Harvard Business School in 2002, Immelt described the results: "I think we stink in Europe today."

THE HUB STRATEGY

Companies seeking to add value at the regional level frequently begin by adopting this strategy. Originally articulated by McKinsey consultant Kenichi Ohmae, a hub strategy involves building regional bases, or hubs, that provide a variety of shared resources and services to local (country) operations. The logic is that such resources may be hard for any one country to justify, but economies of scale or other factors may make them practical from a cross-country perspective.

Hub strategies often involve transforming a foreign operation into a stand-alone unit. In the early 1990s, for instance, Toyota began producing a limited number of locally exclusive models in its principal foreign plants—previously a taboo—thereby signaling the company's intention to build complete organizations in each of its regions. These plants thus started to serve as regionally distinct hubs, each with its own platform, whose products were designed for sale within the region.

In its purest form, a hub strategy is simply a multiregional version of the home base strategy. For example, if Zara were to add a second hub in, say, Asia by establishing an operation in China to serve the entire Asian market, it would shift from being home based to being a multiregional hubber. Therefore, some of the same conditions that favor a home base strategy also favor hubs. It should also be noted that multiple hubs can be very independent of one another; the more regions differ in their requirements, the weaker the rationale for hubs to share resources and policies.

A regional headquarters can be seen as a minimalist version of a hub strategy. After the European Commission blocked GE's merger with Honeywell, GE felt the need to dedicate more corporate infrastructure and resources to Europe, partly to attract, develop, and retain the best European employees and partly to acquire a more European face for political reasons. In 2001, therefore, GE switched from a portfolio to a hub strategy by establishing a regional HQ structure in Europe—complete with a CEO for GE Europe. The company followed up in 2003 by establishing a parallel organization in Asia.

The impact of the typical regional HQ is limited, however, by its focus on support functions and its weak links to operating activities. For example, the regional presidents within Wal-Mart International perform a communication-and-monitoring role, but otherwise their influence on strategy and resource allocation seems to be mainly personal. In any event, a regional HQ is seldom a sufficient basis for a regional strategy, even though it may be a necessary part of one. (See the insert "A Regional HQ Is Not Enough" at the end of this article)

The challenge in executing a hub strategy is achieving the right balance between customization and standardization. Companies too responsive to interregional variation risk adding too much cost or sacrificing too many opportunities to share costs across regions. As a result, they may find themselves vulnerable to attacks from companies taking a more standardized approach. On the other hand, companies that try to standardize across regional hubs—and in so doing overestimate the degree of commonality from region to region—are vulnerable to competition from local players. Thus we see Dell, whose product is relatively standard across its regional operations, forced to modify its plans in China to respond to local companies competing aggressively on cost by producing less-sophisticated, lower-quality products.

THE PLATFORM STRATEGY

Hubs, as we've seen, spread fixed costs across countries within a region. Interregional platforms go a step further by spreading fixed costs across regions. They tend to be particularly important for back-end activities that can deliver economies of scale and scope. Most major automakers, for example, are trying to reduce the number of basic platforms they offer worldwide in order to achieve greater economies of scale in design, engineering, administration, procurement, and operations. It is in this spirit that Toyota has been reducing the number of its platforms from 11 to six and has invested in global car brands such as the Camry and the Corolla.

It's important to realize that the idea behind platforming is *not* to reduce the amount of product variety on offer but to deliver variety more cost-effectively by allowing customization atop common platforms explicitly engineered for adaptability. Ideally, therefore, platform strategies are almost invisible to a company's customers. Platforming runs into difficulties when managers take standardization too far.

Let's look again at the automobile industry. Sir Nick Scheele, outgoing COO of Ford, points out, "The single biggest barrier to globalization [in the automobile industry] . . . is the relatively cheap cost of motor fuel in the United States. There is a tremendous disparity between the United States and . . . the rest of the world, and it creates an accompanying disparity in . . . the most fundamental of vehicle characteristics: size and power." This reality is precisely what Ford ignored with its Ford 2000 program. Described by one analyst as the biggest business merger in history, Ford 2000 sought to combine Ford's regional operations—principally North America and Europe—into one global operation. This attempt to reduce duplication across the two regions sparked enormous internal turmoil and largely destroyed Ford's European organization. Regional product development capabilities were sacrificed, and unappealingly compromised products were pushed into an unreceptive marketplace. The result: nearly $3 billion in losses in Europe through 2000 and a fall in regional market share from 12% to 9%.

THE MANDATE STRATEGY

This cousin of the platform strategy focuses on economies of *specialization* as well as scale. Companies that adopt this strategy award certain regions broad mandates to supply particular products or perform particular roles for the whole organization. For example, Toyota's Innovative International Multi-purpose Vehicle (IMV) project funnels common engines and manual transmissions for pickup trucks, SUVs, and minivans from Asian plants to four assembly hubs there and in Latin America and Africa, and then on to almost all the major markets around the world except the United States, where such vehicles are larger. Similarly, Whirlpool is sourcing most of its small kitchen appliances from India, and a host of global companies are in the process of broadening the mandates of their production operations in China.

As with platforms, the scope for mandates generally increases with the degree of product standardization around the world, even though the mandate strategy involves focused resource deployments at the regional and local levels. But interregional mandates can be set up in some businesses that afford little room for conventional platforms. For instance, global firms in consulting, engineering, financial services, and other service industries often feature centers of excellence that are recognized as repositories of particular knowledge and skills, and are charged with making that knowledge available to the rest of the firm. Such centers are often concentrated in a single location, around an individual or a small group of people, and therefore have geographic mandates that are much broader than their geographic footprints.

There are of course several risks associated with assigning broad geographic mandates to particular locations. First, such mandates can allow local, national, or regional interests to unduly influence, or even hijack, a firm's overall strategy: More than one professional service firm can be cited in this context. Second, broad mandates cannot handle variations in local, national, or regional conditions, which is why the near-global mandate for Toyota's Asian pickup engine and transmission plants excludes the United States. And finally, carrying the degree of specialization to extremes can create inflexibility. A company that produces everything based on global mandates would be affected worldwide by a disruption at a single location.

The reader will have noticed that Toyota figures as an illustration in all the foregoing descriptions. Indeed, this is because Toyota provides perhaps the most compelling and complete example of how the effective application of regional strategies can produce a global powerhouse. The success is apparent: Toyota surpassed Ford as the world's second-largest automaker in 2004 and is poised to overtake General Motors in the next two to three years. The exhibit "The Toyota Way" reproduces a slide that the company uses to summarize the evolution of its strategy. It shows both that Toyota looks at strategy through a regional lens and that it has, in fact, progressed through all the strategies I've just described.

What is also interesting about Toyota is that new modes of value creation at the regional level have supplemented old ones instead of replacing them. Although Toyota has moved beyond a Japanese manufacturing base (the home base strategy), exports from Japanese manufacturing facilities to the rest of the world continue to account for more than one-quarter of the company's volume and a significantly larger share of its profits. In regions other than the two in which it has strong

The Toyota Way

This exhibit is an almost exact reproduction of a slide presented to Toyota investors at an informational event in New York City in September 2004. The only change I have made is to label the slide to highlight how the various elements identified in the Toyota strategy correspond to the five strategies described in this article. Toyota's "global network," which combines all the other approaches, can be considered a sixth strategy.

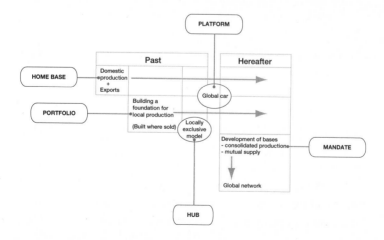

positions—East and Southeast Asia and North America—
Toyota is still following a portfolio approach. In terms of
regional hubs, the promotion of a production and procurement specialist to succeed Fujio Cho as president
signals an increased commitment to transplanting the
Toyota Production System from Japan to the newer production hubs at a time when overseas production is
being ramped up rapidly. But even as its hubs gain
strength, Toyota continues to reduce the number of its
major production platforms and pursue additional specialization through interregional mandates. The IMV
project described earlier plays a critical role in all three
respects.

The picture that emerges is not one of Toyota pro-
gressing through the various regional strategies one at a
time but of a company trying to cover all the bases. One
can even argue that the application of all five regional
strategies itself represents a new form of strategy—the
"global network" in Toyota's slide—in which various
regional operations interact with one another and the
corporate center in multiple ways and at multiple levels.

Of course, Toyota's ability to employ a complex mix of
regional strategies to create value is inseparable from the
company's basic competitive advantage: TPS's ability to
produce high-quality, reliable cars at low cost. Without
this fundamental advantage, some of Toyota's coordination attempts would drown in a sea of red ink.

Defining Your Regions

As companies think through the risks and opportunities
of various regional strategies, they also need to clarify
what they mean by the word "region." I have so far
avoided a definition, although most of my examples

imply a continental perspective. My goal is not to be elusive but to avoid restricting the strategies to a particular
geographic scale. Particularly with large countries, the
logic of the strategies can apply to intranational as well
as international regions. Oil companies, for example,
consider the market for gasoline in the United States to
consist of five distinct regions. Other large markets
where transport costs are relatively high in relation to
product value, such as cement in Brazil or beer in China,
can be similarly broken down.

The general point is that one can interpret the
regional strategies at different geographic levels. Assessing the level—global, continental, subcontinental,
national, intranational, or local—at which scale is most
tightly tied to profitability is often a helpful guide to
determining what constitutes a region. Put differently,
the world economy is made up of many overlapping geographic layers—from local to global—and the idea is to
focus not on one layer but on many. Doing so fosters
flexibility by helping companies adapt ideas about
regional strategies to different geographic levels of
analysis.

In addition to reconsidering what might constitute a
geographic region, one can imagine being even more creative and redefining distance—and regions—according
to nongeographic dimensions: cultural, administrative
and political, and economic. Aggregation along nongeographic dimensions will sometimes still imply a focus on
geographically contiguous regions. Toyota, for instance,
groups countries by existing and expected free trade
areas. At other times, however, such definitions will yield
regions that aren't geographically compact. After making
its first foreign investments in Spain, for example, the
Mexican cement company Cemex grew through the

rest of the 1990s by aggregating along the economic dimension—that is, by expanding into markets that were emerging, like its Mexican home base. This strategy created the so-called ring of gray gold: developing markets that mostly fell in a band circling the globe just north of the equator, forming a geographically contiguous but dispersed region.

At times, the parts of a region aren't even contiguous. Spain, for example, can be thought of as "closer" to Latin America than to Europe because of long-standing colony-colonizer links. Between 1997 and 2001, 44% of a surge in FDI from Spain was directed at Latin America—about ten times Latin America's share of world FDI. Europe's much larger regional economy was pushed into second place as a destination for Spanish capital.

Finally, it's important to remember that the definition of "region" often changes in response to market conditions and, indeed, to a company's own strategic decisions. By serving the U.S. market from Japan, Toyota in its early days implicitly considered that market to be on the periphery of its own region. The North American West Coast was easy to access by sea, the United States was open to helping the Japanese economy get off the ground, and the company's business there was dwarfed by its domestic business. But as Toyota's U.S. sales grew, political pressures increased the political and administrative distance between the two countries, and it became apparent that Toyota needed to look at the United States as part of its own self-contained region.

Leading-edge companies are starting to grapple with these definitional issues. For example, firms in sectors as diverse as construction materials, forest products, telecommunications equipment, and pharmaceuticals have invested significantly in modern mapping technology,

using such innovations as enhanced clustering techniques, better measures for analyzing networks, and
expanded data on bilateral, multilateral, and unilateral
country attributes to visualize new definitions of regions.
At the very least, this sort of mapping sparks creativity.

Facing the Organizational Challenge

Regional strategies, as I've noted, can take a long time to
implement. One deep-seated reason for this is that an
organization's existing structures may be out of alignment with—or even inimical to—a superimposed
regional strategy. The question then becomes how best
to mesh such strategies with a firm's existing structures,
especially when the established organizational players
command most of the power.

For some pointers, consider Royal Philips Electronics,
which has been a border-crossing enterprise for virtually
all of its 114-year history. Philips's saga not only points to
alignment challenges but also reminds us that regionalization is rarely a triumphal march from the home base
to interregional platforms or mandates.

Starting in the 1930s, Philips evolved into a federal
system of largely autonomous national organizations
presided over by a cadre of 1,500 elite expatriate managers who championed the country-oriented approach.
But as competition emerged in the 1960s and 1970s from
Japanese companies that were more centralized and had
fewer, larger plants, this highly localized structure
became expensive to maintain. Philips responded by
installing a matrix organization—with countries and
product divisions as its two legs—and spent roughly two
decades trying, without much success, to rebalance the
matrix away from the countries and toward the product

divisions. Finally, in 1997, CEO Cor Boonstra abolished the geographic dimension of the matrix as a way of forcing the organization to align itself around global product divisions.

Given this long and sometimes painful history, it would be unrealistic for today's champions of regional strategies within Philips to expect to overthrow the product division structure. Would-be regionalists have to work within it. Jan Oosterveld, who served as CEO of Asia Pacific from 2003 to 2004—a position created after Philips announced the combination of two Asia Pacific subregions into one—saw that his first task was to facilitate the sharing of resources and knowledge across product divisions within the region. Ultimately, however, he aimed to help develop an Asia Pacific strategy for the company. So although the new Asian regional structure has initially focused on coordinating governmental relations, key account management, branding, joint purchasing, and IT, HR, and other support functions, Oosterveld and others can imagine a day when much more power might be vested in regional headquarters in, say, New York, Shanghai, and Amsterdam than at the corporate level. They also recognize, however, that achieving that kind of regional strategy could take many years.

The obvious implication is that strategic initiatives can be pursued at the regional level only if some decision rights are reallocated—whether from the local or global levels, or from the other repositories of power within the organization (in Philips's case, product divisions). And just as obviously, no one likes to give up power. Leadership from the top, aimed at promoting a "one-company" mentality, is often the only way forward. One of Oosterveld's conditions for taking the job at Philips was that the board of directors hold regional conclaves twice a year to show its commitment to the regional initiative.

Such conclaves might be mainly symbolic, but symbolism can go a long way.

Philips has approached regional strategy flexibly, putting in place a wide variety of arrangements that take into account not only the company's existing structure but also competitive realities, region by region. In North America, for example, Philips's principal objective continues to be to rebuild its positions and achieve satisfactory levels of performance in the all-important U.S. market. Its activities there are organized entirely around the global product divisions, which, because of the size of the market and Philips's stake in it, are thought to be capable of achieving the requisite geographic focus.

In Europe, where Philips is better established, the company has rethought the role and status of the large operations in the home country of the Netherlands within the broader regional structure. In April 2002, when Philips announced plans to set up a regional superstructure in Asia Pacific, it also folded the Netherlands into an expanded region comprising Europe, the Middle East, and Africa. The point is that irregular or asymmetric structures (in which some regions seem to be much larger than others) are often preferable to an aesthetically pleasing (and in some respects simpler) symmetry of the sort implicitly evoked by much of the discussion up to this point. Even Toyota seems to be focusing separately on China while its other markets are grouped into multicountry regions.

If your company has a significant international presence, it already has a regional strategy—even if that strategy has been arrived at by default. But given the variety of regional strategies, and the fact that no one approach is best or most evolved, there is no substitute for figuring out which ways of coordinating within or across regions make sense for your company. As we have seen, however, embracing regional strategies calls for flexibility, creativity, and hard-nosed analysis of the changing business context—all of which take time and effort.

In a highly regionalized world, the right regional strategy (or strategies) can create more value than purely global or purely local ones can. But even so, the regional approaches I have been exploring may not make sense for your company. In that case, here is what you can take away from this article: Regions represent just one way of aggregating across borders to achieve greater efficiencies than would be achievable with a country-by-country approach. Other bases of cross-border aggregation that companies have implemented include products (the global product divisions at Philips), channels (Cisco, which uses channels and partners as its primary basis), customer types or global accounts (many IT services firms), functions (most major oil companies), and technologies (ABB recently, before and after trying some of the bases that are listed above and others that aren't). Each of these bases of aggregation offers, as regions do, multiple possibilities for crafting strategies intermediate to the local and global levels by grouping things. In a world that is neither truly local nor truly global, such strategies can deliver a powerful competitive advantage.

A Regional HQ Is Not Enough

MANY COMPANIES with explicitly global ambitions have reacted to the regionalization of the world economy by establishing a set of regional headquarters. This kind of organizational response has, in fact, also been the focus of most of the management literature on regions. Michael Enright, for example, has described some interesting patterns in recent articles in the *Management International Review* on the functions performed by regional management centers. But to focus on regional HQs or any other organizational structure as *the* primary object of interest is a little like focusing on the briefcase rather than its contents. Without a clear sense of how a regional structure is supposed to add value, it is impossible to specify what the structure should try to achieve. A company with no regional HQs may still use regions as the building blocks of its overall strategy, and a company with many regional HQs may still not have a clearly articulated regional strategy. In other words, having regional headquarters doesn't mean that you actually have a regional strategy.

Is a Regional Strategy Right for Your Company?

TAKE A COUPLE of minutes to complete this short questionnaire. First, circle one option for each of the following eight categories. Then complete the scoring. Give yourself −1 for each "a" response, 0 for each "b" response, and 1 for each "c" response, and then add up the numbers. A positive score may indicate a significant need for strategy at the regional level. The higher the score, the greater is your need.

Of course, this kind of questionnaire is no substitute for analyzing your company's situation—and regionalization options—in detail. But if the results prompt you to look at your regional strategy more carefully, the exercise will have been useful.

COMPANY FOOTPRINT

Number of countries with
significant operations   SCORE

a. 1–5
b. 6–15
c. >15   _____

Percentage of sales from the home region

a. >80%
b. 50%–80%
c. <50%   _____

COMPANY STRATEGY

Objective for interregional dispersion

a. Decrease
b. Maintain
c. Increase   _____

Number of bases of aggregation
(or grouping) to be pursued

a. 1
b. 2
c. >2   _____

COUNTRY LINKS

Percentage of trade that is intraregional

a. <50%

b. 50%–70%

c. >70%   _____

Percentage of FDI that is intraregional

a. <40%

b. 40%–60%

c. >60%   _____

COMPETITIVE CONSIDERATIONS

Differences in profitability across
regions

a. Small

b. Short-term

c. Long-term   _____

Key competitors' strategies

a. Deregionalizing

b. Unchanged

c. Regionalizing   _____

TOTAL SCORE   _____

Scoring	− 1 for each (a) response
	0 for each (b) response
	1 for each (c) response

Notes

1. For a systematic way to think about cultural, administrative, geographic, and economic distance, see the CAGE
   framework described in my article "Distance Still Matters:
   The Hard Reality of Global Expansion" (HBR September
   2001).

Originally published in December 2005
Reprint R0512F

About the Contributors

JOSEPH L. BOWER is Donald Kirk David Professor of Business Administration at Harvard Business School with 44 years of research and expertise in strategy and organization, resource allocation, and the changing role of the leader. He founded The General Manager program and currently serves as Chair of The Corporate Leader program at Harvard Business School and is on the Board of Directors of several corporations.

CLAYTON M. CHRISTENSEN is the Robert and Jane Cizik Professor of Business Administration at Harvard Business School, with a joint appointment in Technology and Operations Management and General Management. He is the author of *The Innovator's Dilemma* and *The Innovator's Solution* for Harvard Business Press, as well as numerous other books and articles.

PETER F. DRUCKER was a writer, teacher, and consultant. His thirty-four books have been published in more than seventy languages. He founded the Peter F. Drucker Foundation for Nonprofit Management, and counseled thirteen governments, public service institutions, and major corporations. He is the author of many books and articles including *Peter F. Drucker on the Profession of Management* and *People and Performance* for Harvard Business Press.

JOHN J. GABARRO is UPS Foundation Professor of Human Resource Management, Emeritus at Harvard Business School. He is the author of *Managing People and Organizations, Dynamics of Taking Charge,* and *Breaking Through: The Making of Minority Executives in Corporate America* with David A, Thomas for Harvard Business Press.

PANKAJ GHEMAWAT is the Anselmo Rubiralta Professor of Global Strategy at IESE Business School in Barcelona and the Jaime and Josefina Chua Tiampo Professor of Business Administration (on leave) at the Harvard Business School. He is the author of *Redefining Global Strategy* and numerous articles for Harvard Business Review.

GARY HAMEL is Visiting Professor of Strategic and International Management at the London Business School; cofounder of Strategos, an international consulting company; and director of the Management Innovation Lab. He is the author of *Leading the Revolution* and coauthor of *Competing for the Future*. He has also written numerous articles for *Harvard Business Review,* the *Wall Street Journal,* the *Financial Times,* and many other business publications.

ROSABETH MOSS KANTER is the Ernest L. Arbuckle Professor of Business Administration at Harvard Business School, specializing in strategy, innovation, and leadership for change. She advises major corporations and governments worldwide, and is the author or coauthor of fifteen books, including *Evolve!: Succeeding in the Digital Culture of Tomorrow* (HBS Press, 2001).

JOHN P. KOTTER is the Konosuke Matsushita Professor of Leadership, Emeritus, at Harvard Business School, and is widely regarded as the world's foremost authority on leadership and change. He is the author of many books, including the international bestsellers *A Sense of Urgency, Leading Change,* and *Our Iceberg Is Melting.*

MICHAEL E. PORTER is the Bishop William Lawrence University Professor at Harvard Business School. He is the author of seventeen books and numerous articles. He is the leader of the Institute for Strategy and Competitiveness at Harvard Business School. He is the author of *On Competition, Redefining Health Care,* and numerous articles for Harvard Business Review.

C.K. PRAHALAD is the Paul and Ruth McCracken Distinguished University Professor of Corporate Strategy at the University of Michigan's Ross School of Business. He has consulted many of the top companies internationally. He is the author of *Harvard Business Review Classic: The End of Corporate Imperialism, Competing for the Future* and numerous articles for Harvard Business Review.

H. EDWARD WRAPP was a professor of business policy at the Graduate School of Business, University of Chicago, a position he held for 20 years. He was director of the school's executive program and associate dean for management programs. He also served on the board of numerous corporations.

Index